Indiscretions of
The London Boulevardier

*Excerpts from an
Artist's (so-called) Life*

Francis Charlton

Volume 4
Arty Bollocks

Indiscretions of
The London Boulevardier

Excerpts from an
Artist's (so-called) Life

Francis Charlton

Volume 4
Arty Bollocks

For Mrs Peeps

'All work and no play makes Dave a dull boy.'

'Ivanka! I'm home.'

(Thanx to Stanley Kubrick and Michael Stipe)

Excerpts from an Artist's (so-called) Life

Patisserie Valerie

Alan opens the Daily Mail exclaims 'Fuck me!'
And turning to our waitress says, 'Quick, I
need a pair of triple espressos! Followed by a
pair of triple espressos. Grazia'
'What is it?' I ask.
'Spanish.' Says Alan. 'Thanks.'
'For what?'
'Er...for asking.'
'No. What did you read? And why the fuck the
Daily Mail?
'Dave.'
'Yes Alan.'
'I've forgotten.'
'Forgotten what?'
'What you were asking.'
'He was asking,' says AK SE1©, 'What you
were reading.'
'Er...the menu?' Says Alan.
'No, after the menu.' Says Wanksta© dipping
a croissant into his espresso.
'Er...'
'Alan.' Says Ms Metro, 'We want to know what
it was you were reading about?'
'Oh! Now I remember.' Says Alan.
'Good.' I say, 'Share it.'
'Share what?' Says Alan.
'Do me a fucking favour!' Susie says, slapping
the newspaper down in front of Alan. 'What
the fuck were you reading about?'
'It's about your exhibition Dave,' Alan says
opening the paper.

Excerpts from an Artist's (so-called) Life

Artist arrested for ABH on Art Critic

'And I quote,' says Alan:
'Dave the (so-called) London Boulevardier and contemporary artist was arrested last night at the opening of his latest show of new work. Dave, the only painter among a lacklustre short-list for last year's Turner Prize, had dismissed, out of hand, the nomination, citing he was *'Bored by it. So terribly, terribly bored.'*
Witnesses allege that Dave launched an unprovoked attack on Art Critic AGD rendering him insensible. Mr and Mrs Witness, of Crouch End, were travelling on the top deck of the number 38, and were able to see the altercation after wiping the window free of condensation. Mr Witness, who had left his bifocals at home, was able to describe the incident with the help of his wife. 'Well I looked out and saw what appeared be two geezers fighting in the middle of the road. Ethel said, ' There's a dark skinned gentleman hitting a poor immigrant. Eastern European, I think. I could tell by his accent. He was shouting things like, *'mindthecoiffure!* and *'Ohnonotthebarnet!*

Acquaintances of the Witnesses say they are a lovely couple, able to enjoy life again now that they have a replacement guide dog. Their previous dog met with a tragic accident after having been trapped in their fan assisted oven, at 180f for 50 minutes. Mrs Witness said, 'I wouldn't have eaten him if I'd known.'

Friends of the acquaintances of the Witnesses say that Ethel and Tom will require therapy for the foreseeable future, and their dog Bengy no.4, would benefit from animal psychiatry.

AGD was rushed from the scene to a branch of Trevor Sorbie, where he was attended to by a team of stylists under the supervision of Mr Sorbie. AGD was released at 10am the following morning. He thanked the waiting Crowds. Phil and Pauline Crowd said, 'Well, he came over to us and looking closely into Phil's mirrored sunglasses said, *'Because I'm worth!'* Phil, I tell you, felt honoured.'
A spokesperson for the Metropolitan Police said that no charges were brought and the incident was now closed. The spokesperson confirmed that Dave, was granted diplomatic immunity when the Russian Cultural Attaché arrived at the Gallery. Mr Ivanko, apparently, invited Dave to sit with him in his bullet and bomb-proof, tinted windowed, one kilometre per gallon, Diplomatic limousine, while his Gallerist Clive and the chief art buyer for the Russian Cultural Institute, rumoured to

relative of his, and girlfriend of Dave, Ivanka negotiated with the Police.

The spokesperson for the London Ambulance Service confirmed that they and the Police were already at the Gallery, having responded to an emergency call. She also confirmed, that artist, DF had crucified himself for attention. DF was subsequently taken to the Richard Dadd Memorial Hospital for Tired and Emotional Artists. He is being detained under Section 136 of the Mental Health Act 1983, for 72 hours, to enable an assessment of his current mental state to be made. The spokesperson went on to say that his incarceration was voluntary and he could, in fact, discharge himself whenever he chose to.

Clive, Dave's agent and owner of two galleries, he opened his Mayfair gallery when he was still a student at the LSE in the mid-70s, his Shoreditch gallery opened on the back of Dave's, highly praised, first exhibition ten years ago, was at the scene.

He was asked to comment on the events. Clive said, 'Not since the days of Jake and Dinos has the art world been as vibrant and colourful as it is now. Dave and his fellow artists known in art circles as 'the Usual Suspects,' were keeping alive the Bohemian tradition of working hard at their art and partying equally hard! Although we will draw a line under other, alleged, activities.'

When pressed on exactly what was he alluding to, Clive said, 'It is well documented that amongst the creative communities that due to their temperaments, artists, actors, poets etc. often push the boundaries of what is socially acceptable behaviour.'

Clive gave examples of this behaviour, describing what many readers of this newspaper will find abhorrent. Acts of self-destruction, involving alcohol and drug misuse, irresponsible sexual behaviour involving same sex couples, BDS+M, which this newspaper will not lower itself further into the gutter to explain. Sexual acts involving family members, minors and farm animals. Sleeping with their life models before painting them. Dave, when asked about an alleged peccadillo involving his girlfriend and his models, declined to speak to us. Although, it was pointed out to this reporter that he allegedly said. 'I can't listen to any-more of this provincial nonsense. I'm bored! So terribly, terribly bored.' And that he had been asleep on his feet for the previous 50 minutes.

Michael Hoare, Art Critic for the Kulture Section of the Sunday Times, known for his scathing opinions on contemplating art, reviews Dave's latest exhibition. Michael who did not attend the exhibition, places it in context on pages 10, 11, 12, 13, 17, 18, 19...'

Alan closes the paper, and folding it in half, sets fire to it and lights up his Wandsworth Wonder, a spliff the size of the Common. Taking a drag and exhaling seven minutes later he tries to focus on Ms Metro sitting next to him.

Rubbing his eyes he taps her on the shoulder saying, 'Wanksta© pass this to Ms Metro will you?'

'I'm Ms Metro. You half-wit!'

'Ms Metro's taking a shit? She didn't tell me.' Alan says looking baffled.

'I don't have have any mitts.' Says Susie looking at her hands.

'But what great tits!' Alan says, reaching out to touch Susie's breasts.

'How you say?' Asks Vincenzo, 'She will have fit..?'

'I'll have a bit.' Says AK SE1©.

'The pair of you are looking to get hit!'

'You tell them Susie. What a pair of gits.' Says Nine Mil Phil© looking smug.

Alan toking on his 2Ws, points to Susie saying, 'get your kit off Ms Metro.'

Ms Metro hits Alan with a basket of Brioche.

'That's Susie...'

'This is the pits,' I say, 'Where's the wit?' Realising what I said, I think it's time to take my leave. Slipping a perfectly folded £50 note into our waitresses hand, I exit onto Old Compton Street with a flourish saying, 'I quit!'

'You're a legend Dave,' Wanksta© shouts after me, 'A fucking legend.'

Excerpts from an Artist's (so-called) Life

Strolling up Dean Street, a waft of freshly
baked garlic bread accosts me like a $20
hooker in cheap stilettos, who emerging from
an alley on a wet Fall evening, in down-town
Minneapolis, smelling of stale perfume and
blowing smoke from her four pack a day
habit into my face, says, 'Wanna fuck me?'
'Lunch.' I think. 'Pizza and a small case of
Peroni to start. Followed by anti-pasta of garlic
bread, salad topped with garlic dough balls a
main course of a pair of Fiorentina pizzas, with
a brace of Peroni's. And, maybe a chocolate
bomb and a Margarita pizza for dessert. But!
Which branch, Greek Street or Coptic Street?'
Flagging down a black cab and leaning into
the cabbies window, I say, 'Pizza Express.
Greek Street or Coptic Street? What do you
think my old son?'
'Well squire,' says a Eastern European with no
fixed accent. 'Coptic Street innit!'
'!?!?!?'
'It's a no-brainer squire. The Greek Street
branch is 30 seconds away. The Coptic Street
restaurant 15 minutes, which I can stretch to
35-40 minutes by not running lights, and
letting other taxis out of side streets. It's what
we London cabbies call a 'nice little earner.''
'Fascinating,' I say. 'If only I'd been listening.'
Opening the cab door I get in and exit through
the opposite door, and into a taxi that had
just dropped off a party of Legal secretaries
on a Soho pub crawl. 'Coptic Street.' I say.

'No problem,' says the cabbie, 'hold on tight!'
Bouncing off the pavement, we circle Soho
Square three times, hit Charing X Road and
without slowing down drive the wrong way up
Denmark Street where we lose the other black
cab.

'Eat my exhaust!' The cabbie shouts into his
rear view mirror. 'Anyway, what did you do to
piss him off?'

'He tried to be a geezer, but he tried too
hard.'

'Say no more.' Says the cabbie entering into
the line of traffic.

Three minutes later we pull up outside Pizza
Express. Getting out I pass him a perfectly
folded £20 note, saying, 'Keep the change,
my son.'

'Cheers!' He says. 'But before you go, aren't
you that painter geezer who's been in the
news all day? They say you hit some ponce of
a critic.'

'Yes.' I say. 'Yes. I am. However, let me correct
two points the tabloids are alleging happened,
in order to elucidate what may be a better
understanding of the situation. Firstly, Critics
are fair game. Point two, Critics are fair
game.'

'Aren't they the same?' The cabbie queries.

'Good point.' I say, 'Point 2.1. It was a choke
hold, and not as reported, me trying to
remove his head from his body.'

'Fox News is reporting that policy failures of
the Obama Administration has led to disorder
and violence on the streets of capital cities
around the world, and last night was the

latest example of this. President Obama was not able to comment, when asked why he had not attended your opening.'

'You've done your homework.' I say backing towards the restaurant.

'I'm a London cabbie, ain't I? Gotta keep abreast!'

As he heads towards Gower Street, I head towards a window table and...

Excerpts from an Artist's (so-called) Life

'...fuck me!' Says Clive, 'what are you doing here?'

'Apparently waiting for you to leave so I can have this window table.'

'Why don't you join us?' Deborah *'Yes Master'* Slur says, looking every inch a bad secretary. 'Let me get you a drink.'

'Thanx,' I say, as she gets up to accost a waiter.

'Sorry we couldn't be more supportive last night, we had to rush off.'

'Clive!?!?!! What the fuck are you talking about?'

'Oh! Deborah is not my only new signing to the Agency, she's also my new secretary, and, er, girlfriend?'

'Erm!?!?!?!!'

'And in her rôle as secretary she'd forgotten to invite an influential foreign buyer. And as my girlfriend she'd dressed provocatively in latex to incite other men's attention, particularly yours Dave. Therefore I had to take her back to my apartment, to do, er, stuff?'

'Stuff Clive?'

'Yes Dave stuff.'

'What stuff Clive?'

'Er, you know? Stuff.'

'Clive?'

'Yes Dave?'

'This, what Deborah would laughingly call a conversation, is about to render me comatose. I am very, very bored. However, if you vacate your table, I move my hand to my Mock Glock, you will, perhaps, live to mount another exhibition.'

'The table is yours Dave. Deborah and I are going to the Gallery to read your reviews.'

As Clive gets up, Deborah rejoins us, 'I'll meet you at the car. Opening her Kelly she takes out a matte black Chanel lipstick. As she puts on the lippy she watches Clive leave the restaurant in her mirror.

'Dave. Can we talk?'

'No Deborah.'

'It's important Dave.'

'Why Deborah?'

'It's about Clive.'

'What about Clive?'

'He wants to be you.'

'Me?'

'You.'

'Why me?'

'Blimey?'

'No Deborah. Why me?'

'Fly me?'

'No. Why me?'

'Doh ray me?'

' Deborah, this is like trying to have a conversation with Alan. You have until the waitress standing next to me returns with my pre-starter, starter, to explain what the fuck it is you want to tell me.'

'I'm going to dump Clive, and I'm returning to Berlin on the early evening flight.'

'Please elucidate.'

'He thinks he can be you, with the magnetism that attracts women. He doesn't have a clue.

I've become his trophy S+M girlfriend. Would you give him this?'
Passing me a white envelope with a black border,' she says, 'I'm off to the bathroom. And Dave?'
'What Deborah?'
'If you think I've been bad, why don't you take me to your studio and teach me a lesson?'
'I don't think so Deborah. I suggest you leave now and take the envelope with you.'
I give her the envelope as my pre-lunch, lunch is being served and as Clive re-enters the restaurant.
'Hi Dave, sorry to disturb you, but...oh! Hi Debbie. I thought you...'
'Enough of this nonsense!' I say. 'Clive Deborah has something for you. Read it, then put her in a taxi to the airport and come and join me for lunch.'
As Clive takes his seat our waitress serves our lunch, six bottles of Peroni each, and a pair of Margarita pizzas to start. 'Are these for me?'
'Yep!' I say.
'Thanks Dave,' says Clive picking up a whole pizza and Peroni in each hand. She's dumped me! She says...'
'I know Clive, and I'm already bored by it.'
'But...'
'Clive we require more pizzas and Peroni's'. Nodding to our waitress I order twelve Peroni's and four Fiorentina pizzas, six garlic breads, and six salads with extra house dressing.
'That should do to start,' I say, 'however, we require three more Peroni's each as an aperitif with eight bowls of olives on the side.'

The waitress looks up from her pad, cogitates for a moment and says, 'You're Dave, the artist everyone's talking about.'
'Yep! And you are?'
'Kathy, an aspiring actor with designs on the West End and life model at Goldsmiths.'
'Interesting,' I say.
'Um!' Says Clive.
'Let me introduce you to my agent and Gallerist, Clive. Clive Kathy. Kathy Clive.'
'Hi Clive.'
'Um...' says Clive.
'My Dog! This is banal, so banal the prospect of narcolepsy brings with it sweet relief. Kathy!'
'Dave?'
'Would you like a private tour of my exhibition?'
'Yes please. Love to.'
'What time do you finish your shift?'
'In five minutes.'
'Good. Clive is going to forsake his second lunch, and personality show you around the exhibition. He may also give you a signed poster. Clive is then intending to organise a gathering of the *Usual Suspects* in One Aldwych. Where we'll drink cocktails and talk arty bollocks. Would you like to join us?'
'Yes please. I'll go and get changed.'
'Kathy before you go, can you make sure all the Peroni's and food are delivered to my table. I'm feeling a little peckish. And Kathy?'
'Dave?'
'Are you ever bad?'
'I can be. Why do you ask?'

'Clive will explain...'
'Er, is it true what I've read?'
'Clive will explain.'
'Because I can be very bad.'
'Clive will explain, won't you Clive?'
'Um..!' Mutters Clive.
'As Kathy leaves to get ready, I say to Clive,
'For fucks sake! Be a little more assertive. I've laid a foundation, it's now up to you to build on it.'
'Okay Dave.'
'And Clive.'
'Get the fuck away from my table!'
As five waitresses serve me my lunch, I watch through the window, as Clive and Kathy drive off towards the East End.

Excerpts from an Artist's (so-called) Life

Leaving the waitress with a perfectly folded £50 tip. I think, 'home for a shower and change before talking bollocks with Alan and the *'Usual Suspects.'*' I decide to walk to my apartment via Wagamama in Soho, as I'm still a little peckish. I order three bowls of Yasai Yaki Soba, six Sapporo's and two cheesecakes as an appetiser. While I'm waiting I check my messages:

'You have eight new messages and no saved messages. First message. 'Dave, it's Deborah. I fly out at 9.30 this evening and as you know only too well I've been bad. I'm staying at the Radisson and I have everything you need here if you want to discipline me. Ciao!' Message deleted. Next message. 'Dave, it's Deborah do I need to remind you that I've been bad? You know where to find me.' Message deleted. Next message. 'Dave, would it help you to focus on my lack of obedience, if I said, I am after all Deborah Slur.' Message deleted. Next message. 'Dave, it's Deborah...' Message Deleted. Next message. 'It's Deb...' Message deleted. Next message. 'Dave, it's D...' Message deleted. Next message. Message deleted. Next message. Message deleted. You have no more messages.'

As my noodles are being served my cell vibrates and plays *La Wally,* after letting it play through I answer, 'Are you wearing a blue dress?'

'Dave?'

'Birgit?'

'Yah, Alan has invited me to join you and the, er, Usual Suspects this evening. I would love to arrive there.'

'Be there. Birgit.'

'Ah yah! Sometimes my English is not so good.'

'Your English is good. *Be there* was my recommendation.'

'Yah, I understand. Tac. Where are you?'

'Slurping my last bowl of noodles. Where are you?'

'I am sitting in Golden Square enjoying the ambience. It is a different, er, ambience. I have been spending most of morning and afternoon with AGD, who is asking me to interrupt with you...'

'Intervene, Birgit.'

'Tac Dave. Intervene – between you and him, to ensure success of documentary.'

'Birgit?'

'Dave?'

'You are one minute away from my location and five away from my apartment. Stay where you are while I eat my cheesecakes, and I'll come to you and we'll discuss this over a bottle of Pinot Grigio and a bowl of Alfonso olives.'

'Okay. Tac.'

Excerpts from an Artist's (so-called) Life

Strolling through Berwick Street market, we
fondle the fruit, and banter with the market
traders.
'A lavely pair of coconuts...'
'Tac,' says Birgit, ' they are pert yes?'
'He means the coconuts.' I say.
The trader looks at me and says, 'Did I?'
'Did you what?' Birgit queries.
'Mean the coconuts,' says the trader.
'Your coconuts?' Asks Birgit.
'No your breasts,' says the now pissed off
trader who in an effort to regain his 'Jack the
Lad' attitude, says, 'If your boyfriend don't
mind. Do you want to fondle these coconuts?'
'Your balls, yah!' Says Birgit leaning over the
cabbages, arms outstretched like a zombie
lurching towards brains.
The trader steps back, shielding his groin,
slips on a rotten tomato and lands in a box of
citrus fruit.
'Oranges and lemons say the bells of St.
Clement's my old son.' I say.
'Do what?' Says the trader, struggling to get
up, 'you're having a facking laugh!'
'Yah,' says Birgit your Mockney Cockney
'Eastenders' humour is good.'
'Do me a facking favour luv. I'm the real
thing.'
'He's the real thing,' says Birgit pointing to
me.
'Tac,' I say, 'shall we boulevard to my
apartment?'

'Could we investigate the licensed sex shops on our way there?'

'Yes,' I say, 'yes indeed.'

'Then yah, let us boulevard...'

'What about my coconuts?' Shouts the incensed trader.

'A colourful part of London, with such interesting people,' laughs Birgit.

As we reach the end of Berwick Street, Birgit's hand tightens on my arm, and she says, her voice a little lower, 'Look Dave there is an *Agent Provocateur.* Introduce me..?'

Excerpts from an Artist's (so-called) Life

We are buzzed in by...
'...Hi Dave,' says Naomi.
'...Naomi Hi. We require a fitting. This is Birgit.
Birgit Naomi. Naomi Birgit.'
'Hi Birgit, any thoughts on what you're looking for?'
'Yah definitely, I ideas have.'
'Okay let's take your measurements. Dave are you waiting?'
'Nope, I'll wait in the Carlisle Arms on Bateman Street, which Birgit needs directions to, unless you'd like to join us for a drink?
'Love to...' Naomi winks, 'and?'
'Yes Naomi, put the purchases on my account.'
Forty minutes and eight pints later I'm joined by Naomi and Birgit each carrying two large pink bags.
'Hello,' I say, 'don't I know you two?'
'Yes Dave you do. Naomi was very helpful, my new underwear is so tight it fits like a mitt.'
'Glove,' I say.
'Yah, fits like a gauntlet?'
'Glove!'
'Yah, I understand. It fits like a pair of Marigolds.'
'?!!!!?'
'Moving on,' Naomi says, 'why don't we have a drink and then back to your apartment to model the underwear?'
'Done. And done,' I say, turning to the bar geezer...

'Good evening, Mr Torrance.'
'Hi Lloyd,' I say, 'been away, now I'm back.
'Good evening, Mr Torrance. It's good to see you.'
'It's good to be back, Lloyd.'
'What'll it be, sir?
'Hair of the dog that bit me.'
'Eight pints of London Pride?'
'That'll do her,' I say.
'No charge to you, Mr Torrance.'
'No charge?'
'Your money is no good here. Your, if I may say so, antics keep us amused. It's the least that we can do.'
Birgit and Naomi look at each other quizzically.
'And Lloyd,' I say, 'could you get whatever these two want, whoever they are.'
Ordering a Black, and a White Russian each, Birgit turns to me at the exact moment I start to slide down the bar.
'Dave! Are you alright?'
'Am I upright? Clearly not,' I say, looking up at her knees. But I am downright turned on by the thought of you and Naomi modelling your new underwear...'
'Shall we go then?'
'Go where? I say a little perplexed.
'To your apartment?'
'Why?'
'So we can show off our underwear.'
'Ah!' I say, 'why would you want to do that?'
The bar geezer, meanwhile, has passed two pairs of pints down to me.
'Enough.' Naomi says 'We're taking him

home.'

Lifting me by the arms, they carry me to the street. 'It's not that far,' Naomi says, 'I've been before.'

'Let's have that,' Birgit says taking the pint out of my left hand, which I allow her to do as it gives me time to finish the pint in my right hand.

'As an artist,' I slur, ' I notice things. Case in point. You two have grown about a metre taller, whilst I am shrinking.'

'It's because you're lying on the pavement Dave. Let's get you home,' says Naomi, lifting me to my feet.

Excerpts from an Artist's (so-called) Life

Fifteen minutes later we're standing outside the door to my apartment.

'There's a tramp lying across your doorstep,' says Naomi with a look that is best described...no, can only be described as disgust, crossing her face.

'A piss smelling, gutter dwelling, society rebelling...er, vanker, I think you call them,' says Birgit.

'I heard that,' says Martin rolling over to face us, 'and I am offended.'

'Hi Martin, good to see you.'

'Good to see you too Dave. But I do not like the company you are keeping.'

'You know this street derelict?' Says Naomi, looking aghast, pointing to Martin.

'Indeed,' I say, 'Indeed I do. Martin has been protecting my doorway for a number of years. And, if I may say, and I will, doing a fine job of it.'

'Thank you Dave . It is good to be appreciated.'

'My doorway, like any doorway, in any Metropolis, anywhere in the world, is often used as a toilet,' I explain, 'Martin protects the sanctity of my sanctuary.'

'I am always there for you, Dave.'

'And I am there for you too. Now, would you like to come in, shower and join us for dinner?'

'Yes Dave, it would be my pleasure.'

Birgit and Naomi exchange glances of...

'Fear! Your two friends have got the fear Dave. And I think that I am the cause of it.'
'You may be Martin, you may be. But you are also the cure.'
Birgit and Naomi throw each other looks of...
'Bemusement! They have no idea what you are talking about. Perhaps, Dave, you should elucidate the situation to put them at their ease, while I have a shower and..?'
'Yes,' I say, 'yes indeed. Help yourself to anything in my wardrobe, while I, taking your sage advice, will attempt to ameliorate their discomfort. I Indeed I will. Come join me in the parlour, choose a chaise lounge and before your intimate fashion show, I will explain, if I don't get bored with the explanation, Martin's journey from *Master of the Universe* to piss soaked protector of doorways via existential angst through paranoia to keeper of the secret(s) of the eye(s). Join me, if you will, on this journey, the quest where one man discovers that money is the root of all evil, and that nothing changes, only the individual.'
Birgit and Naomi look...
'Bewildered,' says Martin, resplendent in a crushed green velvet smoking jacket, black linen trousers, black carpet slippers and white pirate shirt. 'They do not, I am afraid, understand your referencing Rod Serling. Perhaps we should forget the narrative of my life and concentrate on dinner?'
'You are not wrong Martin, you are, in fact, correct.'

'I take that as a compliment Dave. Why don't I...'
Martin is interrupted by my cell phone blaring out Fat Les, '*Na Na Naa, Na Na Naa, Na Na Na,*' ' knit one, pearl one,' I say.
'Dave?'
'It is I.'
'Dave?'
'Yes Alan.'
'Oh!'
'..?'
'We're waiting for you in the cocktail bar.'
'F.A.B.' I say
'..?'
'I'm,' I continue.
'Yes Dave.'
'On.'
'On what Dave?'
'My.'
'Your what?'
'Way. Alan. I'll be bringing an entourage with me.'
'The more the Maid Marion.'
'?Alan?'
'The more the Sherwood Forest.
'Alan?'
'Yes Dave.'
'Alan.'
'Yes.'
'What the fuck are you talking about?'
'Er. The more the Robin the Hooded Man.'
'Alan.'
'Yes Dave.'
'What are you trying, and so obviously failing to articulate?'

'?'

'Alan.'

'Dave.'

'Alan.'

'Dave.'

'I said, I'm going to be bringing some people with me. Were you perchance, looking for words of encouragement?'

'Er?'

'Alan.'

'Yes Dave.

'Alan.'

'Dave.'

'Alan. Were you going to say, the more the merrier?''

'Dave.'

'Alan.'

'You're bringing merry men with you?

'No Alan. Naomi, Birgit, who you'll remember from my opening night, and Martin. The more the merry-men to talk arty bollocks.'

'You mean these men are pissed?'

'What men?'

'The merry ones.'

'What merry ones.'

'The merry ones you're bringing with you?'

'Alan.'

'Dave.'

'Alan.'

'Dave.'

'Alan, we'll see you in ½ hour, after we've eaten some snax.'

'Who'll see me?'

'Me and the boys.'

'I thought you were bringing men?'

'It's an expression Alan.'
'Er..?'
'Like the usual suspects?'
'That's what they call us.'
'I know.'
'What do you know?'
'I know I'll be there in ½ hour.'
'Be where?'
'In the cocktail bar.'
'Which one?'
'The one you're in.'
'In Turin, are you with Vincenzo?'
'No Martin and...'
'You're drinking Martini in Turin with Vincenzo.'
'Alan.'
'Dave.'
'Alan.'
'Dave.'
'Is Ms Metro with you?'
'Who?'
'Your girlfriend.'
'What girlfriend?'
'Sorry Alan, I mean fiancé.'
'You're going to flambé my girlfriend? '
'Alan.'
'Dave.'
'Alan.'
'Dave.'
'Is the woman you're going to marry with you?'
'I'm marrying my flambéed girlfriend? Isn't she likely to be in a coma?'
'I know, I know it's serious...'
'What?'
'Sorry Alan, I couldn't resist.'

'You found my girlfriend irresistible. I thought you were my best friend?'
'Alan.'
'Dave.'
'Alan.'
'Dave,
'Is there a woman sitting next to you?'
'Yes.'
'Is it Ms Metro?'
'Yes.'
'She is the person you're going to marry...'
'I'm getting married?'
'Yes.'
'To Ms Metro?'
'Yes Alan, and I'm your best man.'
'Dave.'
'Alan.'
'Dave.'
'Alan.'
'Does Ms Metro know?'
'Know what?'
'She's getting married?'
'Er..!'
'To me.'
'Alan.'
'Dave.'
'Would you please pass the 'phone to Ms Metro.'
'You want me to pass the 'phone to Ms Metro?'
'Yes Alan.'
'Why Dave?'
'So I can talk to her.'
'You're going to chat up my girlfriend, the woman I'm going to marry?'

'Alan.'
'Dave.'
'Alan.'
'Dave.'
'Give the goddamn 'phone to Ms Metro!'
'Who?'
'For fuck's sake Alan...' at which point I'm prodded in the ribs by Naomi.
'Put the 'phone down and let's eat.'
'A good idea,' I say, 'a very good idea. Alan we'll see you later.'
'Let us partake of some sustenance and get to know each other,' says Martin passing a plate of olives and ciabatta to Birgit.
'Tac,' says Birgit looking deeply into the eyes of Martin, who returns the look.
'Mmmmm!' I think.
'Mmmmm!' Says Naomi.
'Let's cancel the the lingerie show,' I say, 'we'll eat and join the usual suspects for an evening of nonsensical conversation.'
'We concur,' says Naomi, taking me by the elbow and leading me towards the kitchen.
'?'
As we pass Martin and Birgit, I overhear Birgit say 'Martin I may have got you all wrong...'
'Okay,' I say to Naomi, 'now I understand. Martin?'
'Yes Dave?'
'Naomi and me are going straight to One Aldwych, you and Birgit eat the food, enjoy the wine, and if you want to join us we'll see you later...'

Excerpts from an Artist's (so-called) Life

As we enter the lobby of One Aldwych the manager approaches us. 'Hello Dave, good to see you.'

'You too Quentin.'

'Can we have a word about Alan, privately?'

'Yes,' I say, Naomi you join the usual suspects and I'll see you later.'

'Okay.'

'Let's get a drink?' Quentin says, leading me towards the restaurant bar.

'Yes,' I say, 'yes indeed?'

The barman smiles as we enter.

'Hi Lloyd,' I say, 'a little slow tonight, isn't it?'

'Yes, it is, Mr Torrance. What'll it be?'

'I'm awfully glad you asked me that, Lloyd. Because I just happen to have two twenties and two tens right here in my wallet. I was afraid they were gonna be there until Alan borrowed them. So here's what, slip me six pints of London Pride, followed by a chaser of six pints of London Pride. You can do that, can't you Lloyd? You're not too busy, Are you?'

'No, sir, I'm not busy at all.'

'Good man! You set them up and I'll knock 'em back, Lloyd. One by one, 'white man's burden,' Lloyd, my man, white man's burden. Say, Lloyd put this on my tab will you?'

'On your tab it is, Mr Torrance.'

'That's swell. I like you, Lloyd. I always liked you. You were always the best of them. Best goddamn bartender from Timbuktu to Portland, Maine or Portland, Oregon, for that matter.'

'Thank you for saying so.
Here's to an evening of talking arty bollocks
with the usual suspects, but you know Lloyd,
things could be better, things could be a
whole lot better.'
'I hope it's nothing serious.'
'No nothing serious. Just a little problem with
Alan. Nothing I can't handle, though, Lloyd.'
'Artists. Can't live with them. Can't live
without them.
'Words of wisdom, Lloyd. Words of wisdom.' I
say as I leave the bar.
'I think, Quentin, we may have sojourned into
the *Twilight Zone*! A, Kubrick's Kube if you
will, an alternate reality, oh my brother, only
to be repatriated before the snow closed
down all access in or out.
'You're not far off the mark Dave. However,
Alan seems to be trapped in his own version,
with no apparent egress.'
'Tell me more, Quentin. Tell me more.
However, be aware I may fall asleep with
boredom!'
'Well since he and the usual suspects arrived,
he's been talking to himself.'
'Nothing new there, Quentin.'
'And answering himself back?'
'Par for the course,' I say.
'And forgetting everyone's names?'
'Nothing unusual!'
'Forgetting he's marrying Ms Metro?'
'I'm getting bored now Quentin.'
'Forgetting who he is?'
'So bored. So terribly, terribly bored?'
'Forgetting he's an artist?'

'Now that is serious Quentin. That is serious indeed, let us repair to their table.'
Leaving a neat stack of perfectly folded £20 notes on the bar, my attention is diverted by the bar geezer trying to catch my eye.
'A drink on the house?' He suggests.
'I'm tempted Lloyd. What do you recommend?'
'In a voice suddenly guttural, he says,
'RedRum! RedRum!'
'No thanx,' I say, 'I prefer white rum.'

Excerpts from an Artist's (so-called) Life

'Yo!' I say as I walk into the Cocktail Lounge.
'Dave!' Says Wanksta©.
'Dave!' Says Nine Mil Phil©.
'Dave!' Says Colin 45©.
'Who are you? Says Alan.
'For fuck's sake!' Says Ms Metro sighing.
Sitting next to her, I order two bottles of
Prosecco. 'The bubbles will help,' I say.
'The plot and Alan have parted company,'
says Ms Metro. 'He thinks his ability to create
art will be lost when we have the baby. He's
smoking too many WWs to avoid thinking or
talking about the situation.'
Alan, I notice appears to be consumed in the
task of carving **'DADA'** into the tabletop.
'Perhaps,' I say, 'he hasn't come to terms with
his impending fatherhood?'
'He's terrified, he thinks his life and his art are
over, so he's seeking oblivion through getting
high, but in fact, it's only making him forgetful
and more absent minded than usual?
Alan meanwhile is singing to himself, *'Up, up
and away in my beautiful balloon.'*
Ms Metro taking a large glug from her bottle
says 'Alan! Dave's here to see you.'
Alan stops singing, and, slowly turning to look
Ms Metro full in the face say, *' Here's Johnny!'*
'You mean Alan.' Says a clearly incensed Ms
Metro.
'Who's this Alan? ' says Alan.
Ms Metro stands up grasping two empty
bottles of Prosecco and calmly says, ' The

baby only requires one parent, two is a bonus. Your gravestone, Alan, will read: ' *He never made it through the first trimester.'*

As she lifts the two bottles above her head she is kettled by Wanksta©, Vincenzo, Nine Mil Phil©, and AK SE1© who slowly march her to the exit. As they pass me Wanksta© says, 'He's all yours Dave. Call if you need us..!'

'Alan' I say.

'Dave.'

'Alan.'

'Dave.'

'Here's the thing...'

'I can't hear a ring.'

'Alan.'

'Dave.'

'Here's the thing.'

'Is it the ringing of the bells?'

'What bells?'

'Can't you hear them?'

'What?!?'

'They're tolling in my head!'

'Alan.'

'Dave.'

'Alan. I'm going to talk. You Alan, are going to listen.'

'We're going on a mission?'

'Mother...'

'We're going undercover?'

'... Fucker...'

'We're going undercover as truckers?'

'Alan.'

'Dave.'

'Alan.'

'Dave.'

'Shut the fuck up! Don't say another word. Remain stumm. Zip it. Do not utter a fucking word.'

'!?!'

'Here's the thing. We believe, that is me, Ms Metro and your close friends, that your unusually bizarre behaviour is a product of your failure to embrace fatherhood. To accept that you and Ms Metro are going to have a baby. You believe your art will be lost, that you will be unable to create, that your muse has deserted you and left you devoid of talent, and because of this erroneous thinking, you are losing yourself in a dope cloud. One that you can't see into or see out of. It's time to get a grip and take responsibility for your behaviour. You are not losing your talent, in fact, your artistic potency is magnified. This is your greatest creation, a collaboration of creativity. You, Alan, have made a *baby!*'

While Alan cogitates over this, I pour myself a large glass of Prosecco. And another. Then another. Three bottles later, Alan starts to grin.

'Alan?'

'I understand,' says Alan, 'I am a God! I, a found sculpture artist, have achieved the ultimate, I have found my Godhood. And I have created life. Only Victor Frankenstein before me was as successful...I always thought I moved in mysterious ways, but the reason was a mystery to me until now. Tell Ms Metro I'll see her at home this evening.'

'Where're you going Alan?'

'The Embankment?'
'Why?'
'I'm going to cross the Thames on foot?'
'Hungerford Bridge?'
'No, on the water!'
'You're going to walk on water?'
'It's what Gods do Dave.'
'Alan?'
'Dave.'
'Alan.'
'Dave.'
'Do not say a fucking word! You have smoked your last joint. Do you want to find yourself in a locked ward of the Richard Dadd Memorial Home for Tired and Emotional Artists, with other, if I may be blunt, crazy, fucked-up, schizo ever so slightly psycho so-called artists. Do you want to share a bathroom with DF? Or Hammer? Well do you?
'Fuck me,' says Alan, suddenly clear eyed, 'you've certainly made your point.'
'Good.' I say, 'it's time to embrace your responsibilities and say no to schmoking excessive amounts of WWs, or at least until the baby's first birthday.'
'Dave you are...'
'...correct and insightful as always,' says Martin sitting down with Birgit.
'Hi Martin,' I say, glad you've joined us and you too Birgit, Alan and me were just discussing art and fatherhood.'
'Tac,' says Birgit, we know, we were listening and Martin was making notes.'
'Making notes?'

'Yes Dave, Birgit has offered me a position as her assistant. I have been telling her about my experience looking into the abyss and how you helped me overcome my fear.' Martin suddenly stops, looks around and shouts out **'Harold!'** And looking sheepish says, 'Well nearly all my fears?'

'Have you...' I start to say.

'Yes,' says Martin looking at Birgit, 'I've told her everything, she accepts me as I am.'

'Yah.' Says Birgit, 'and I have informed Martin on everything with me. Including my love of tight underwear and spanking.' Birgit looks at Martin with a slight blush.

Alan starts to breath heavily, he either wants a schmoke or Birgit or both. Noticing us looking at him, he says, ' A dad, can you Adam and Eve it?'

'Yes,' says Ms Metro sitting next to him and kissing him with...

'...some pash', says Wanksta© joining us. 'Hey Martin, sorry, don't stop.'

'And I have suggested Dave,' says Martin looking at Birgit, 'that as you are a master of the art, she should attend your studio when required.'

'Thank you Martin,' I say.

'It is my pleasure,' says Martin, 'thank you.'

'No,' says Birgit, 'I thank you both.'

'No really,' I say, 'I thank you.'

'No, I thank you,' Says Martin.

'No really, I thank you,' I say.'

'No. I thank you Dave.'

'No. Really. I thank you Martin.'

'Ah!' Says Birgit, 'this is what has been described as *'the Usual Suspects talking arty bollocks nonsense.''*

'Alan,' I say, Birgit wants to talk arty bollocks...'

'She wants to frolic? Whatever will Ms Metro say?'

'Alan, are you saying Birgit wants Ms Metro in the hay?' Wanksta© queries.

'Today?' Says Nine Mil Phil©, 'I'll be there.'

'Where?' Asks Vincenzo.

'I'm taking a chair,' says Alan.

'But what to wear?' Queries Birgit.

'I really don't care,' states Martin, 'go as you are.'

'Take whose car?' Asks Alan.

'This could go on all night,' I think. 'Excuse me,' I say, heading towards the bathroom.

'Ah!' Says Birgit, 'and this is what has been described by AGD as Dave's exit strategy. A phenomenon that occurs when Dave experiences situations which are so boring, inept and mind-numbingly pedestrian that he considers self-harm or elective defenestration. Dave, to protect what's left of his sanity, takes the quickest way out. Which is usually through a toilet/bathroom window.'

'It's true,' I say, 'so very, very true.' And with a wave. A flourish actually, I walk to the loo. Five minutes later I'm on the Strand, leaning into a taxi window saying take me to...'

Excerpts from an Artist's (so-called) Life

'...Borough Market, my son,' says the cabbie. 'Thanx squire,' I say tipping him a perfectly folded £20 note. Walking into the Rake I catch the eye of bar geezer, saying, 'that table in the corner, one chair and bring me every German beer you sell.'
'You got it man.'
'And...' I say, 'if anyone asks, I'm not here.'
'Yep. But you should know, that the art critic you tried to strangle, and I quote from the latest issue of *'artpimp'* magazine.'
I notice an open copy on the bar top. 'You've started, you may as well finish.'
'Artist commits ABH on AGD outside of TSB. Saying you can bank on this, you mo**** fu****. Before trying to trepan him with a palette knife.' He's been in here to film background shots, and enquire if any of our regulars would share anecdotes about you with him for the documentary he's making. So far no-one's said anything, well that's not wholly true, I've overheard comments.'
Fuck knows why, but I ask anyway, 'such as?'
'Most of the replies were short and sweet, *'Get fucked!' 'You must be having a laugh!' 'Is that a can of Elnet in your pocket or are you just pleased to see me?' 'Cover the mirrors! Cover the mirrors before it's too late!'* And it goes on...'
'...and on,' I say, 'and I realise that I did ask the question. However spare me the details.'
'You got it!' Says the bar geezer.

'And if anyone asks. Remember, that's me in the corner, that's me in the dim light, losing my objectivity.'

'Okay,' says the bar geezer looking decidedly nervous and edging towards the relative safety of the bar.

'Consider this, Lloyd,' I say, 'consider this. They say *happiness is a warm gun,*' well my concealed Mock Glock is at the right room temperature to lay waste to a small army of mercenaries and, through what the Military call collateral damage, everyone in the bar. So Lloyd, be warned! Do you want all these potential casualties on your conscience.'

'Oh! Okay!' Says the bar geezer.

'And Lloyd!'

'Yes.'

'I like you Lloyd, I've always liked you. Why don't you come home with me and you can fuck my sister?'

There is a thud as he vaults the bar counter and lands heavily on the other side. He sticks his head up and rests his chin on a beer coaster. With his left eye twitching and his right blinking uncontrollably, he throws a worried, if not slightly deranged look to the customers and says, 'please be aware that Dave is in the bathroom!'

My cell vibrates to the music of Johann Strauss. Opening the flip I say, ' I have no idea,'

'...Dave. It is Ivanka. By Lenin's goatee, what are you referring to with your lack of knowledge?'

'The black monolith,' I say, 'what was it.'

'Comrade Kubrick is waltzing with your head. Uncle Joe would surely approve, and he would subsequently redact his approval to further mess with you. While you, Comrade Dave, wait for a cold bed in a Gulag, like it was your Christmas present.'

'Ivanka.'

'Dave.'

'You rang me!'

'Yes Dave, by Lenin's polished visage I did. I am in need of your attention, my tight black panties require removing by strict spanking.

'Have you been bad Ivanka?'

'Yes Dave, very bad.'

'What have you done?'

'Nothing. But I will think of something.'

'Fine by me,' I say, be at my studio at midnight and wear your bridesmaids dress?'

'By Putin's lack of shirts, there is nothing missing in your thinking Dave. I will be there Comrade, and I may be tardy?'

Closing the flip I notice the table is now laden with German bottled beer. 'I'll start with the blondes and finish with a dark, evocative, and sultry little number, that has spent too much time in a dark smoky beer Keller and is longing for the open air of a Bavarian beer garden. 'I don't think so,'' I say to the bottle as I pick it up, noticing the condensation I flip the stopper. I put my lips on the neck, licking the initial foam away, I saviour the dark heady and malty aroma for a moment, and, looking straight at the bottle, I put my tongue into the opening and drink deeply. 'Arhh! The taste of it!' Realising I'd been speaking out loud, I look around and I'm greeted by spontaneous applause.

'Even in a quiet reflective moment, away from the intensity of being a leading figure in the contemporary London art scene, Dave the London Boulevardier displays his erotic magnetism. When he's relaxing the spotlight is rarely off him...'

'For fuck's sake,' I say as AGD and his camera crew approach my table...'

'...the opportunity presents itself,' continues AGD, without missing a beat, 'to interview Dave in an unguarded moment...'

'...unguarded! You must be fucking joking, you must be having a laugh, you're a joker, a fucking comedian. If I wasn't going to weaponise this saucer of dry roasted peanuts, I would probably chuckle, perhaps even chortle, maybe manifest an indiscreet giggle. I may have to hold my sides, with tears running down my face, as the laughter consumes my whole body. You are wasted as an art critic, have you considered stand-up comedy? You could headline the Comedy Club, Stephen Fry would quake in his boots, shake in his gloves, and gesticulate to his agent to shoot him, having realised his career is now over.' Picking up the heavy saucer of nuts, I advance towards AGD, who flicking his hair out of his eyes, steps behind a sound engineer who says, 'I can see Dave's point, you're having a fucking laugh,' and deftly steps out of the way.

As I raise the saucer, Alan steps in front of me, 'Is this a fucking ballet?' I ask as he picks out a dry roasted nut and places it on his tongue and slowly masticates. 'Ermmm, I think we require a table and a brace of pints to help wash these nuts down. Bar geezer a brace of Erdingers for the table in the corner, a chair, and would you show the door to AGD.'
'Yes,' says the barman clearly relieved.
'No need.' Says AGD, I can show myself out.'
Only stopping to check his reflection in the bar window AGD exits leaving his crew drinking at the bar.
'A round of Erdingers for the crew,' I say as the bar geezer delivers our drinks. Turning to Alan I say, 'What are you doing here?'
'Sharing quality time with you. What you said to me earlier this evening...'
'... I have no idea what I said, I rarely listen to other people talking, let alone listen to what I'm saying.'
'Anyway, I appreciate it. You talked mucho sense, it's brought me back to reality, this is why you're my best friend.'
'And our best man,' says Ms Metro, sitting on Alan's lap.
'Alan leaning towards me asks, 'Do you know this woman?'
For a moment Ms Metro is not sure, slowly she starts to smile,'You learned that deadpan expression off Dave. You don't fool me.'
'Dave who?' Asks Alan.
'Ms Metro starts to snigger, giggle and convulse with laughter, 'Oh I need to pee,'

she says pointing at us. It's good to see you're your old-self Alan?'

'Who's Alan?' Says Alan looking at me.

Ms Metro, meanwhile has rushed to the loo laughing like a hyena.

'I could keep this up all night,' Alan says looking mischievous.

'But you won't,' I say.

'No,' says Alan.

'I needed that,' says Ms Metro, taking a seat at our table, 'I wanted to say 'thank you' Dave, for being there for us...'

'...me too,' says Alan, 'you're a diamond geezer...'

'Bored now,' I say, 'so terribly, terribly bored. Shall we move the conversation on and discuss wedding plans, or do I exit through the bathroom window?'

'Well, Ivanka's got her bridesmaids dress,' says Ms Metro.

'Yep,' I say, 'we're art going to preview it tonight.'

'What about your attire?, she continues taking out an iPad to make notes on.

'The flying helmet and goggles arrived by UPS yesterday and the crushed velvet frock coat should be here on Friday?'

'What colour? Asks Alan.

'Orange.'

'Nice,' says Ms Metro, 'it will look striking next to Ivanka's all black ensemble.

'I'm calling it my ' Dandy in the Underworld ' look. A homage to Sebastian Horsley.

'Only you Dave...' says Alan.

'...Yes only you,' confirms Ms Metro.

'However,' I say, before all that there's the premier of Desadia's new film, '*The Artist and the Secretary.*'

'This is going to be interesting,' says Alan.

'Very,' says Ms Metro.

'Yes,' I say, 'yes indeed.'

'I have idea!' Ivanka says pulling a chair up and sitting at the table.

'What happened, and this is rhetorical, to my quiet night of reflection with only a selection of German beer for company?'

'..!'

'..?'

'.!?'

'Exactly,' I continue, 'it has been compromised, thwarted, I may even suggest sabotaged...'

'Comrade!' Says Ivanka.

'Ivanka.'

'Da Dave.'

'What do you want?' I ask, thinking perhaps there's no Russian translation of rhetorical?'

'I have idea.'

'What is your idea Ivanka?'

'I join you for drink?'

'Ivanka!' I say, 'let me explain something to you. Whenever you come in here and interrupt me, you're breaking my concentration. You're distracting me!' I rip up a beer mat and throw onto the floor. 'And it will take me time to get back to where I was! Understand!?

'Da.'

'Fine. I'm gonna make a new rule: whenever I'm...' I feel a tap on my shoulder.

'Dave.'

'Alan.'

'Dave, you're channelling *'The Shining.'*

'You're right Lloyd, er, Alan.' I say. 'Been away, but now I'm back. But seeing as my night of contemplation has been so rudely interrupted, I am now leaving to go to my studio where Ivanka is going to play the lead in *'The Artist and his Bad Girlfriend.'*

Excerpts from an Artist's (so-called) Life

'Don't I know you?' Says the cab driver, winking to Ivanka in his rear view mirror.
'I do not know, Comrade cabbie. I am Dave's girlfriend?'
'Dave?' Queries the cabbie.
'By Lenin's goatee Comrade. He is sitting next to me!'
I nod to the mirror.
'Dave who?' Asks the cabbie turning to look at Ivanka, whilst keeping one eye on the (Tottenham Court) Road.
'He is famous artist. I am his bad girlfriend. No, I redact that statement, I am his **'very'** bad girlfriend. If I do not make amends for bad behaviour, I will be purged and will live out the rest of my life wandering the Serbian steppes, wishing for a cold bed in a distant Gulag.'
'Er...' Says the cabbie.
Tonight Comrade cabbie, Dave the famous artist will play Russian KGB handler. And I, Ivanka, will play an errant spy, who is secretly double agent, and is also bad girlfriend.'
'Do what?' Says the cabbie.
'I can inform you this Comrade cabbie. Under this disguise of a bridesmaids dress which is fabricated in 100% latex, I am wearing tight black underwear. And the only way to remove these bad panties is to spank them off.'
The cabbie, now beaded with sweat says, 'Do me a favour...'
'But Comrade, as double agent, my interrogation will require riding crop to

remove my tight panties before my red striped bum receives the kiss of the whip to teach me the errors of my ways for being double agent and bad girlfriend. But this I will not admit to, so the punishment will be more severe. And Comrade it could go on for hours...

There is a bump as the cab mounts the curb, an Evening Standard vendor jumps out of the way. The cabbie brakes hard, throws his hand-break on and pours a bottle on Evian over his head.

'Fuck me!' He splutters, 'I can't Adam and Eve it. No one will believe me, if I tell them. And I'm trapped behind the wheel by my hard-on...'

'By Stalin's moustache, you need to think about something else Comrade cabbie. You must not think of me tied naked to a cross and lashed mercilessly on my hot and fragrantly sweaty body...'

'No more!' Cries the cabbie.

'That Comrade is what I will say. But Dave will continue to lash me severely until I...'

'Come...!' Shouts out the cabbie collapsing across the steering wheel.'

'By uncle Joe's ubiquitous stare, you understand comrade. But even then I will not be spared, for Dave will start again, because I will beg him to. He will make me count every stroke. And he will start again if I miscount. Let me show you, 48, 49, 17. I always forget what comes after 49. Which, Comrade cabbie, will mean that Dave will have to take out the cat'o'nine tails and give me 50 more lashes..!'

'Urhhhh..!' The cabbie moans sliding off his seat and slumping into the passenger well.
'I think it's time to walk the rest of the way...' I say.
'No charge,' croaks the cabbie, flapping about like a fish in a pool of his own sweat.
'We must make haste,' says Ivanka loudly, 'my interrogation will begin in next half-hour. Do you have ball gag to stifle my cries of pleasure...'
A faint, 'Ohhhhhhh...' Can be heard from the cab.
'As you would say,' smiles Ivanka, 'my work here is done. Let us go now, for I am in need of the real thing.'
'Let us boulevard to my studio,' I say taking Ivanka's hand.

Excerpts from an Artist's (so-called) Life

Thursday afternoon.
The Fountain Restaurant, Fortnum and
Mason.

'We have a booking for an extremely large table,' say Wanksta©.
'What name?' Enquires the Maître de.
'The Usual Suspects,' says Wanksta©.'
'Yes, we have your table. Follow me.'
Having seated us he asks, 'What would you like to drink?'
'Dave?' Queries Wanksta©.
'Well,' I say, 'seeing as there's over fifteen of us, and in all this confusion I've forgotten actually how many are coming, and we don't want to run out before the première this evening, I think we'll have Prosecco. Turning to the waiter, who's sporting a barbed wire necklace and a spiked haircut, I say, 'It's your lucky day. Do you feel lucky? Well do you, PUNK?'
'Yes, I do,' says the waiter.
'Well,' I say, 'are we going for one bottle or two? Call it punk!'
'Two!'
'Good answer. You may have a long career as a waiter ahead of you. Now I suggest you bring us 50 bottles of Prosecco and 40 afternoon teas.'
'But,' says the waiter, 'there's less than 20 in your party.'

Fingering my Mock Glock, I say, 'When I said you may have a long career as a waiter, I should have said, longish.

The waiter clearly nervous, backs into AK SE1©, who whispers, 'Don't push him punk, he's in an Anti-Christ kinda mood, you don't want his vengeance raining down on you.

'N.N.no!' The waiter stutters.

'Leave him with his legs,' says Alan.

'And his arms,' says Nine Mil Phil©, 'but his ears? I'm not sure about.'

'He doesn't need any of them,' says an indignant Susie Uzi.

'How you say? Says Vincenzo, 'take them all. And, take them with extreme prejudice.'

The waiter having reached breaking point, snaps. He jumps over a table and weaving between colleagues and customers exits the restaurant onto Piccadilly and into the arms of an Old Bill, who just happens to be walking past.

'Save me! I need them! I need them all!'

'I'm sure you do Sir. Perhaps, Sir, needs to calm down and breath.'

'Yes!' Says the waiter, 'you're right. Let me use your inhaler...'

'What?' Says the Old Bill.

The waiter grabs the pepper spray from the Old Bill's utility belt and inhales a mouthful, gasping and with tears flooding down his face he sinks to the pavement.

Looking around, the Old Bill, starts to talk to his lapel, 'Emergency. Yes. Responding.' He steps over the waiter and starts to power walk, like fuck, to Green Park.

'We'll never see either of them again,' says Alan, tapping another passing waiter on the shoulder.

'Yes sir?' Asks the waiter.

'Do you want to live?' Asks Alan.

'Er...yes,' replies the waiter, looking at Alan, and fingering a crucifix hanging from his neck.

'Good! Would you please get us 50 bottles of Prosecco and 40 afternoon teas. I thank you and my friends, the usual suspects, thank you too.

The waiter looking a little relieved, says, 'No! Thank you sir.'

'No.' Says Alan, 'Thank you.'

'No.' Says the waiter. 'Thank you.'

'No really,' says Alan, 'I thank you.'

The waiter starts to say something, thinks better of it and says, 'Follow me to your table.'

'Thanx.' I say.

'N...' The waiter thinks better of it, and quietly leaves to place our order.

'The plan,' I say is this. We eat, drink,and when we have reached the point of insobriety, we order more Prosecco and start again. And, if needs be, we start again.'

'Is this anything to do with Deborah Slur joining the Q+A panel, with you and Desadia this evening?' asks Wanksta©.

'You've hit the nail on the head,' I say, 'yes they've changed the time of the panel from 10.30pm, immediately after the film to 7pm, immediately before the film starts, apparently believing I'll require a bathroom break and may not return.'

'Which probably is not far from the truth,' says Alan, considering it's 6.30pm now, we have plenty of time to prepare. I've picked the wrong week to give up spliff. But as your wingman, I'll be there for you.'

'And I agree with Comrade Alan,' says Ivanka, if it becomes unquiet on the Western Front we will push back their advance.' Standing to attention, she clicks her heels, salutes saying, 'we will crush under the treads of our tanks the propaganda of Deborah Slur. Uncle Joe will be proud of us. Although in official reports your names, Comrades, will be changed to good Russian names, such as Boris or Ivan...'

'Ivanka,' I say, 'would you like to sit here with me?'

'Have I been bad Dave?'

'No Ivanka, cuddles.

'As much as I would like cuddles, I think I have been bad.

'No.'

'Yes.'

'Now you're being bad.'

'That is good, yes?'

'No it's bad.'

'But bad is good.'

'Yes, however sometimes good is bad.'

'So, am I good or bad, or bad and good?'

'!!!!!! I need a drink,' I say, shaking my head to clear it ready for question time at the Curzon.'

'I wasn't listening, but I need a drink on your behalf,' says Ms Metro.

'I, too, require a sympathetic drink,' says Alan, ' and perhaps my love, Ms Metro, would programme the number of the Samaritans on my speed dial. I really don't have Dave's resilience, and I've picked the wrong week to give up E's.'

As the food is served, I place an order for 40 more bottles of Prosecco. 90 minutes later, having put the bill on Clive's account, we collectively stagger to the Curzon

'Do you know what time it is?

'No idea,' I say, 'why do you ask?'

'Because it's 8.35 and we should have started at 7.00.'

'Fascinating,' I say, 'started what?'

'The Q&A with the Director and the lead, and you, as you're an integral member of the panel for without you there would be no film.'

'There's a film? I say, 'what times' it start.

'Do you know who I am?

'Absolutely no idea,' I say, who are you?'

'I'm representing the film company on behalf of the Public Relations Firm; *Powers, Productions Produce Positively.* PPPP as we're known in the trade.'

'You're full of PP,' I suggest, 'is *Powers* by any chance Brad Powers?'

'Yes Sir.'

'Indeed, what's your name?'

'Blain. I'm Brads' right hand person.'

'You don't say.'

'I do say.'

'Say what?'

'Excuse me,' says Blain, 'perhaps we should go in and start the Q&A?'

As the Usual Suspects take their, reserved, front row seats, I mount the stage, nod to

Rufus, who is toying with his classic green Pentel roller-ball, and sit between Desadia and Deborah Slur.

'Hi Dave,' says Desadia, 'smiling a smile of wickedness, glad you could join us.'

'Dave...'Deborah says touching my arm, 'have I been b...'

' *Deborah!* Enough.' Desadia snaps.

'...'?!?!!!?' I think.

Rufus coughs for attention, and tapping his Pentel on a clipboard, introduces us to the audience. 'Dave,' says Rufus, 'I think we all know the origins of this film, and as we're a little pressed for time, let's ask the question 'has anyone here not read the Sunday supplements and/or magazines and the stories relating to your guise as the London Boulevardier and the reports of your indiscretions?'

The audience are obviously fans, and no one raises a hand. Rufus continues, 'therefore let us move on quickly. Is it correct to say Dave, that the story behind the film is based on one of your exploits as you avoided putting brush to canvas, as your exhibition date loomed...'

'Getting terribly, terribly bored, I say, 'is there anything to drink?'

'No sorry Dave.'

'No problem,' I say, taking a bottle of Prosecco from an inside pocket and slurping the contents.

Someone in the audience shouts out, 'Yeah Dave!'

'I'll answer Dave's question,' says Deborah leaning towards Rufus, who momentarily out of his comfort zone pushes himself back into his chair. 'That's how I like my men. Subservient and on their knees.' She says this straight to the audience, who stare back blankly.

'Many of you,' says Rufus, taking the opportunity to regain control, 'will remember Deborah Slur as the so-called Arts Correspondent of the now defunct ' *SoWhat!*' Magazine. She is here this evening, because she invited herself?' Leaning forward he whispers, so that even the people in the back rows can hear, 'So shut the fuck up, bitch!' The audience applauds loudly as Deborah slumps back in her chair.

'To continue,' says Rufus, 'Desadia and Dave were the two protagonists in real life, and the film is the story of their brief encounter. Told, if I'm correct in my assessment, having watched the film a number of times, as a love story between two powerful and independent people.'

'I concur with that,' says Desadia.

'And I,' I say taking another bottle of Prosecco out of my jacket pocket, 'would also agree, if I was sober enough to understand what you said.'

'Shall I answer it for you?' asks Deborah.

'I don't think so,' says Desadia.

'Why not? I am, after all, Deborah Slur?'

I feel myself sobering up at an alarming rate. Get me a Goddamn drink!' I shout.

'Me too,' says Rufus, clearly exasperated.

'I hope you don't mind, says Deborah pointing to Rufus, but I've invited AGD to join us...'

'...Who do you think you...' Rufus stops himself short.

Too late.

'I am Deborah Slur!'

'You are indeed,' says AGD climbing onto the stage with a plastic chair and seating himself next to Rufus. 'I'm here at the behest of former arts journalist Deborah Slur. Deborah who is pursuing a career in the field of S+M movies, is currently based in Berlin, and I thank her for being with us tonight. I'm shooting a documentary on Dave the Artist and Boulevardier and she has lent her considerable experience to assist in the making of my film.'

'After all as a former muse to many young and upcoming artists, I am in a unique position to provide insights into their personalities. I championed Dave from the start, giving him both space in the magazine and introducing him to the right contacts to progress his career. I am, after all, Deborah Slur!'

Desadia looks at me and Rufus and whispers, 'Follow me to the Green Room.'

AGD and Deborah continue to massage each other's egos as the lights go down and the film begins. I catch Wanksta's© attention and gesture to him the ' Round them up and move them out ' sign. Three minutes later we're crammed into the Green Room, where Desadia, having opened at least 24 bottles of champagne, hands us two glasses each.

Rufus begins to say, 'I'm...'

'No need,' says Desadia opening four cases of champagne, 'she's getting above herself. She's even claiming that she was the original inspiration for the film…'

'Do me a favour,' says Rufus.

'**Do me a fucking favour,'** I say, 'she needs to be brought down a peg or ten…'

'Dave?'

'Desadia?'

'Breath.'

'Okay.'

'If I may Dave…'

'Yes you may Desadia.'

'Thank you Dave.'

'No really, by that gleam in your eyes I'm going to be thanking you.'

'I believe you've met…'

'…Good evening,' says Man standing next to Desadia.

'That geezer wasn't there a moment ago!' Says a startled Wanksta©.

Vincenzo makes the sign of the cross and faints into the arms of Nine Mil Phil©.

'Hi Man,' I say, ' how's tricks?'

'Good Dave, thanks. Louie says 'Hi, he's loving the last series he bought from you, he says it shows he's a man of wealth and taste.'

'Glad he likes it. Let me introduce you. Man, the Usual Suspects. The Usual Suspects, Man. Man is the custodian of the Hellfire Club and consigliere to Louie Cypher.'

'Enchanté,' says Man, and I swear everyone heard something different.

Vincenzo swoons back into the arms of Nine Mil Phil©.

'Man will explain the *'Extraordinary'* meeting of the Hellfire Club, that has been arranged for this evening.'

'Hello again,' says Man. 'Desadia has requested that Louie open one of the many doors available to him at his Karswell Street residence. And, I can inform you, he is only too happy to oblige.'

'Who's he opening it for?' Queries AK SE1©.

'What's behind it?' Asks Uzi Suzi©.

'How many doors are there...?' Asks Nine Mil Phil©

'Too...' I begin to say.

'Many...' Says Alan.

'Questions,' says Desadia, 'let the man explain.'

'As it were,' I say.

'I return with a renewed Hello! We have been approached to provide a service. To remove an irritant. Desadia has provided us with an opportunity to...' Man's smile appears to cross his face from side to side.

Vincenzo cries out, 'Mamma Mia!' And, this time falls into the arms of Rufus, who with the skill of a pickpocket working Oxford Street on a Saturday afternoon, deftly lifts Vincenzo and places him in the arms of Nine Mil Phil©.

'And he won't know what's happened until he comes to pay the bill in Starbucks,' says Rufus.

'That'll teach the fuckers up from Guildford on a day trip. The fuckers who ask asinine questions, *'Excuse me, can you tell me the way to Oxford Street?'* You're standing on it for fuck's sake. These are the same fuckers who stop dead at the bottom of escalator to consult an A-Z of London, and as the bodies pile-up around them wonder why they're being verbally abused by commuters. Anyway fuck them!!!'

'Wanksta's© on a roll,' I think.

'Goddamn, tourists, they're a fucking nuisance...'

'Hi,' says Man, 'I'm back, and would you believe I haven't actually been away. Now for the sake of brevity, let me cut to the chase, Mr Cypher has a agreed to open a door in the Hellfire cub. Incidentally the meeting this evening is merely a formality, as Mr Cypher sits alone on the Board and only his vote counts. And this door will open onto the Spanish Inquisition and reopen, exactly 14 days later. Albeit the Grand Inquisitor has an option for a further 7 days, should he choose to exercise it.'

'I'm guessing,' says Alan...

'No need to guess,' replies Desadia.

'Hello, I haven't been away!' Man smiles a smile. 'You are all correct in what you're thinking. Yes, the door only opens for...' Man pauses, 'I was going to quote a line from the 'Rocky Horror Show,' but you're all thinking of it anyway.'

There is a collective shiver of an...ti...ci...pation!

'Deborah Slur,' says Man with a gesture of a bow, 'and goodbye, Mr Cypher and myself will see you later this evening.'

'Who said that,' queries Vincenzo.

'That was Man,' replies Nine Mil Phil©.

Vincenzo's eyes roll-up into his head and he appears, although many witnesses believe it was a trick of the light, to float to the floor. Ms Metro and Nine Mil Phil© lift him to a standing position and walk him outside into the fresh air.

'Let us repair to the auditorium and jointhe audience for the final minutes of the film. Lead on Wanksta©, Desadia, Alan and myself will join you momentarily.'

'You have an idea?' Asks Alan.

'Yes.' I say, 'Yes indeed. We require more alcohol for our round table discussion, which we'll hold after the film. The audience will ask questions and whomever is still standing at the end will be Desadia's and my guest at the Hellfire Club at midnight. Alan!'

'Yep!'

'You know what you have to do?'

'Yep, Dave. I will be your plant.'

 So it begins,' I say, 'Avanti.'

Excerpts from an Artist's (so-called) Life

Taking the stage Rufus, Desadia, Deborah Slur, AGD, and myself sit in a semi-circle as the lights go up. Rufus coughing slightly invites the audience to remain in their seats for the Q+A session. 'We have agreed with our guests to answer a number of follow-up questions and then, we the denizens of the night can take our leave, except for Desadia and Dave who are guests of the legendary Hellfire Club, of which little is known, because one cannot separate fact from fiction, truth from untruth. But let us leave rumour and conjecture behind and open with a question for our panel.'

'Hi, I reappear,' says Man, 'is it true that no one knows the location of the Hellfire Club?'

'I can answer this,' I say.

'The question is yours Dave,' Man says with a slight bow.

'You pose an interesting question, which I'll do my best to answer. The address of the club is only made available to those who been invited to attend. And is conditional on absolute discretion. Many have tried (and failed) to ascertain the location of the Hellfire Club, a number of these people were subsequently found living in a box outside of Waterloo Station surrounded by empty bottles of Bulmers, others found themselves on Labour's Front Bench, all of them quite clearly insane.'

'Thanx for the question Man,' says Rufus.

'No, thank you for allowing Dave to answer the question,' says Man.

'Thanx Man,' I say.

There is a cry from Vincenzo of *'Oh, Mama Mia, Mama Mia, (Mama Mia, let me go.) Beelzebub has a devil put aside for me, for me, for me...'* Looking to the sky, he stretches his arms out and resting his head on his shoulder slowly rocks back and forth.

From nowhere Man appears standing in front of Vincenzo's crucifixion pose and says, 'Again, we meet again. But not again for a very long time.'

Vincenzo smiles.

'Dave, Desadia, I'll see you later, and Vincenzo,' says Man, 'I'll see you again.'

Vincenzo, as if on cue, faints into the arms of Nine Mil Phi©, who says, 'I'm taking him home, see you later guys.'

'I think Man was enjoying himself,' says Alan to no one in particular, taking a seat in the front row and raising his hand.

'Yes you in the front row, do you have a question for the panel?'

'If you had a brain Rufus,' smirks Deborah, 'you'd be dangerous. Can't you see that's Dave's friend Alan, the found sculpture artist.'

'How do you know that?'

'Am I not one of the leading authorities on Contemporary Art in this country. I am, after all, Deborah Slur.'

'Moving on,' says Rufus pointing at Alan, 'the floor is yours...'

Alan looking excited says, 'Thank you, I'll be back to collect it later this evening.'

Ms Metro nudging him in the ribs, sighs, saying, 'he doesn't actually mean that, he means you can ask your question.'

'Mr..?' Says Alan to me.

'Dave,' I say.

'Mr Dave,' says Alan.

'Just Dave,' I say.

'Justin Dave?' Asks Alan.

'No Dave,' I say.

'Noah Dave?' Queries Alan.

'Call me Dave.'

'Callum Dave?' Says Alan.

'Dave!'

'I'm Alan.'

'And I'm Dave!'

'Will you both shut up!' Says Deborah Slur, 'None of us finds this juvenile display of repartee amusing...'

'Oh, I don't know,' I say.

'I'm quietly amused,' says Rufus.

'Me too,' says Ms Metro.

'I'm actually laughing on the inside,' says AK SE1©.

'Let's ask the audience,' says Rufus, 'hands-up if you enjoy the dynamic between Dave and Alan.'

The audience raise their hands and sway, creating a Mexican wave that ripples around the auditorium.

'For my sake,' shrieks Deborah, 'this is supposed to be a serious analysis of the Italian soft porn films of the 70s and their influence on contemporary film, especially as it impacts tonight's première of 'The Artist and his Model.' I am here to lend my artistic

67

integrity and my considerable intellect to this evenings performance, as well as my support to the Director Desadia and the Artist Dave, both of whom I mentored to success. They are now, as you would imagine, personal friends of mine. For am I not the well regarded Deborah Slur?'

'And on that note let's ask the audience,' says Rufus, gesturing with open arms, 'embrace the opportunity.'

Wanksta© puts his hand up saying, 'You must be fucking joking Debbie.'

'I couldn't stop laughing when you said, '*Well regarded,*' guffaws Ms Metro clutching Suzi Uzi© to stop her sliding off seat.'

'She's not in control,' says AGD, 'Ignore her, for are you not...'

'Yes I am,' confirms Deborah Slur.

'Am what?' Asks Rufus.

'Yes,' asks Alan, 'am what?'

'Well regarded,' says Deborah smiling at the audience, 'for I am Deborah Slur. Ask AGD I taught him everything he knows. If it wasn't for my mentoring him, he'd still be reporting on the Sunday painters outside of Green Park for some monthly throwaway magazine.

With a glance towards AGD she looks at the audience and snarls, 'don't sit there like dummies, ask him! Demand an answer!'

White knuckled she grips the arms of her chair, as if holding herself back from launching herself at the audience.

Visibly shaking, AGD takes out a can of Elnet and sprays his hair into shape, pulls the nozzle off and inhales the rest. The propellant

works quickly, violently shaking he falls out of
his chair with a cry of *'I'm worth it'* and is
unconscious before he hits the stage.

'See!' Says Deborah, 'how he bows before
me. For I am Deborah Slur.'

Rufus nods to me, Desadia and Alan, coughs,
and says, 'I want to thank our guests this
evening and especially you, the audience.
Thank you and goodnight.'

As the audience file out, Alan says loudly,
'Desadia, for reasons my control, I can't be
your guest at the Hellfire Club the evening.'

'Oh!' Says Desadia, 'you realise this is a
unique opportunity and not to be missed. You
may not be invited again.'

'Er, yes. However, I've been made aware of
some material I can utilise for my found
sculptures and I need to be in on the ground
floor for this. Thank you anyway.'

'Dave, can we take someone else with us?
Desadia asks looking at me, Rufus and Alan as
we huddle talking arty bollocks.'

'Probably not, but that shouldn't stop us,
Rufus, guess where you're going tonight?'

'I accept your invitation, however...'

'There is a high pitched cry of
'Noooooooo!!!!!!!!!!!' from Desadia as she
rushes the stage, and, using the back of a
technician who is bending down repairing a
feed, she vaults over him, her legs part in
mid-air and she slams into Rufus pinning him
to the stage, coming to rest sitting on his
face.

There is a muffled 'Arhhhhhhhhh.'

'Dave, Desadia,' says a slightly winded Deborah Slur, 'I believe I should be your *plus1* at the Hellfire Club. For I am Deborah Slur.'

'Mmmmmm!!!!!!!' Rufus mumbles, although it sounded more like 'Get this clam off my face!!' Grabbing an arm each Alan and myself lift Deborah off and deposit her into a chair. Rufus struggles to his feet, and wiping his face on his sleeve says, 'That was all *'Twenty Thousand Leagues under the Sea.'*

'What do you mean by that?' Queries Deborah. 'What are you implying?'

'Well,' says Rufus, 'I've never been twenty thousand leagues under the sea, nor have I had a woman throw herself at me...'

'Oh!' says Deborah, don't get your hopes up, you wouldn't make the grade if you were the last man on the planet.'

'You are quite the charmer,' says Rufus, 'are you by any chance related to the late Ruby from Rochdale?'

'Will you shut up, you little man! I require the ear of Desadia and Dave.'

'This is going better than expected,' whispers Rufus to Alan and myself.

'Desadia!' Says Alan, 'I don't think Rufus is up to going to the Hellfire Club with you this evening.'

'Man will be disappointed,' says Desadia.

'Not forgetting Louie,' I say, 'he was looking forward to admitting a new member into the Club.'

'He still can, and not a fawning nobody like Rufus. The club requires cachet, people with gravitas, people like me. For, am I not the well

renowned art critic turned international porn star.
I am, she who was famous,
but now is universally famous.
I am Deborah Slur!'
'Sold,' I say, 'you're our guest.'
'Agreed,' confirms Desadia leading us out to a waiting taxi. 'Ciao Alan, we'll leave the tidying to you.'
'Yes you can. In fact, I insist.'
'Later Alan,' I say climbing into the taxi and giving the cabbie a slip of paper with an address on.
'Karswell Street? Er!' Says the cabbie as a sudden wind blows through the taxi and lifts the paper out of his fingers, and, as if it's got a life of its own, it flies around and exits through the passenger window where another gust of wind blows it into a street vendors caramelised peanut cooker, where it shrivels and bursts into flames.

'Er..!' Reiterates the cabbie looking at me.
'Think nothing of it, my good man,' I say, 'think nothing of it'
'I'm, er, not sure where this address is...'
'Head towards Baker Street,' I say, 'I'll direct you from there.'
'This is mysterious, which is how I like my men, mysterious and dominant. Dominant, that is until they meet me and learn subservience, for I am, *'She who must be Obeyed!'*
'The cabbie looks into his rear view mirror and smiles a wry smile and briefly, ever-so briefly,

the face looking at us takes on the visage of Man. And then like an eclipse, it's gone.
'Did you see...' Queries Deborah.
'Yes,' I say, 'yes I did...'
'But??!?!'
'A trick of the light, Desadia, nothing more than a trick of the light.'
'We're coming up to Baker Street,' says the cabbie.
'Turn left and then right and drive up to the private gardens, follow the one-way directions turn right at the pedestrian crossing. Drive along this road until you reach a roundabout. At the roundabout drive around it anti-clockwise, after three circuits take the he sixth exit.'
Driving along a lush tree lined avenue we reach a private road, a black ornate metal gateway blocks the cabs progress.
'Er guv?' Queries the cabbie.
'Leave us here,' I say, tipping the cabbie a perfectly folded £50 note. 'By the time he gets to Oxford Street, he'll have forgotten the last hour.'
'What do you mean by that?' Asks Deborah.
'That by the time he gets to Oxford Street, he'll have forgotten the last hour.'
Desadia pulls a bell on the double fronted gate.
'Hello!' Smiles Man, appearing behind the bars.
'Where did you come from? I demand to know. Do you know who I am?'

'Hello again,' says Man, 'and yes Deborah, I do. You are, in fact our special guest this evening?'

'At least someone knows what they're talking about. Now take me to your leader.'

'I think you mean, 'take me to Louie,' says Man.

'Louie schmooie...'

'No,' smiles Man, 'you mean Louie Cypher. Turning from the gate Deborah looks at us, and says, gesturing towards Man, 'Why is this Chinese houseboy talking to us when he should be showing us in? Does he fail to recognise me?'

'On the contrary,' purrs Man. 'And here I am again! It's as if I haven't been away, and in fact I haven't.' Opening the gate he bids us enter.

Gas street lamps illuminate our path. On either side of the avenue four and five story mansions sit brooding in the semi-darkness, waiting, forever waiting, for their owners to return. Waiting to participate in whatever may unfold under their roofs.

Their wait will not be in vain.

Man bids us to slow down as we approach a Gothic mansion.

'We arrive,' he says walking up stone steps from the pavement to the front door, which opens without him touching it.

'How did he do that?' A bemused Deborah queries.

'Do what?' Asks Man.

'Open the door? How did you do that?'

'It's always open,' replies Man, 'to those willing to enter.'

'Well, I'm always willing. Which begs the question why am I standing outside.'

'After you,' gestures Man, 'and have I mentioned the door is always closed to those wanting to leave.'

'Wanting to leave...?'

'Without paying the price,' says Man.

'The price?' Asks Deborah.

'Of admission,' says Man.

'Which is?' asks Deborah.

'You'll only find out on entering,' Man says walking through the open door.

'Good evening Sir,' says an impeccably dressed man servant. 'Dunhill, Jermyn Street, only after six pm. Ask for Rex, say Dennis sent you.'

'Thanx!' I say, 'you've answered my question.'

'What question?' Says Deborah.

'The one about where Dennis gets his shirts made.'

'Would Sir, and his guests like to follow me to the dining room?'

'You've read my mind,' says Man, 'indeed we would, lead on trusty manservant.'

'Walk this way,' says Dennis opening a double door into a dining room illuminated by candles and a roaring fire, both of which throw dancing shadows onto thick velvet curtains. 'Circa 1897, Holland Park. We liked it so much we decided to recreate the décor and its ambience.'

'Thank you,' says Desadia.

'Is this a cabaret?' Queries Deborah.

'That is to come,' replies Man, for now help yourself to a drink and canapés.'

Dennis shows us to a banquette in a corner, where we are served our drinks and appetisers by tall, voluptuous waitresses dressed in classic Film Noir cigarette tray girl (circa1940) black and white uniforms.

'How may we serve you Dave?' Ask three pneumatic Bettie Page lookalikes speaking in harmony.

'Well...' I start to say...

'Well what? Isn't tonight supposed to be about me?'

'Well, well, well!' Says Man, 'We don't like to share. Do we Deborah?'

'I am the special guest. Don't you people realise that I am Deborah Slur!'

'Hi.' Says Man, 'It is I.'

'Why do you keep introducing yourself?'

'Because, perchance, it is to remind people that I am still here and will continue to be.'

'To be?' Asks Deborah looking confused.

'That I exist,' smiles Man, 'I am the balance, the Alpha and the Omega, the Yin and the Yang, the Black and White, the Good and Bad, the Dis to the Order...'

Deborah attempts to interject, 'What are you...'

'...or it's to curtail the self-explanatory statements you make declaring, usually in the third person, who you undoubtedly are.'

'I am in fact, Deborah Slur, 'and why are you always smiling?'

'You miss the point entirely,' smiles Man. 'I think it's time for the cabaret. This is for you Ms Slur.'

The candles are snuffed and the lights dimmed. There is a loud bang as a spotlight is turned on illuminating a solitary figure in the centre of the stage.

'Hello,' says the figure who is wearing a white suit and appears to glow brighter than the spot.

'Glad you could make it. Dave! Always a pleasure, and Desadia good to see you again...'

Deborah coughs.

Unperturbed the figure continues, '...I am Louie Cypher your host this evening. But enough about me, this is your night Deborah Slur!'

'About time! Let's get on with it,' Deborah snarls, 'you know you need me more than I need you.'

'Your self-importance knows no bounds, and this will be investigated at length during your induction,' Louie smiles and for a moment Man's face appears to superimpose itself over Louie's and It too smiles. Louie takes a slight bow and says, 'But before that, old chums, the Cabaret! No introductions necessary, he's here to sing his first single, released on Monday on the Deviant Vivika label, put your hands together for Former Dictator Vlad Smythz with his version of *Please Release Me.*'

The light goes off and immediately comes back on lighting up a weeping Vlad pulling petals off a red rose and scattering them around him like confetti. Slowly looking up at our table, he, with a catch in his throat, says, 'Ms Slur, this ones for you.'

There is nothing left of the rose but a twig of thorns, which he ties in a band around his head. Holding out his hand, he beckons Deborah to join him the stage.

Deborah throws him a glare and through clenched teeth says, 'This is too ordinary, too working class for a person of my reputation. I am, after all, Deborah Slur.'

Vlad red in the face, and showering spit over Deborah, shouts, ' It's too late! Would you like a last cigarette with your last drink?'

'Whatever are you talking about? Former Dictator, my foot!'

Vlad explodes. 'Bitch! You would have been the first against the wall in my country. You would not be enjoying view hanging upside down from a street lamp...'

Desadia looks at me and whispers, 'This is getting serious.'

'Too late for second thoughts,' I say as the lights go out. We're handed a candle by a statuesque waitress, and as more candles are placed on tables, slowing lighting up the room I notice Vlad and Louie talking.

Louie takes to the stage, the candlelight reflecting off, what appears to be...

'The horn! I'm feeling so horny. So horny in fact, I may need to be restrained tightly and disciplined,' Desadia says, breathing heavily.

'I think I may be the one to administer the release you so obviously deserve.'

'If Ivanka is doesn't mind?'
'I believe Ivanka will expect to participate.'
'Is she good with a spanky stick,' Desadia
asks, panting slightly.
'Yes, I say, but better, so much better with the
cat?'
Desadia tries and to say something but only a
low 'arhhhhhh,' is audible.
'I'm glad that's been resolved,' Louis says
from the stage, 'thank you Dave. Now as our
guest this evening is a little impatient, and
Vlad Smythz has, how shall I say...'
'Spit the dummy,' interrupts Deborah, 'and
yes your guest is impatient, she is not used to
waiting. Waiting is for lesser people, for she is,
is she not, Deborah Slur!'
'You are Deborah Slur,' Louie says pointing at
our table.
'I know who I am,' says a clearly pissed off
Deborah.
'And she, continues Louie, like any tin pot
dictator who is losing his grip on reality, talks
in the third person...'
'I am she who must be obeyed,' says Deborah
interrupting Louie, 'for I am Deborah Slur.'
'You are indeed. And I see your experience
with Desadia and Dave, which resulted in six
paintings for my private gallery, has taught
you nothing...'
'The Devil is in the details,' says Deborah.
'You don't say,' says Louie, and perhaps you
are correct we shall...'
'Move on to my induction to membership of
the Hellfire Club?'
'Am I not moving fast enough for you?'.

'No!' Deborah strikes the table, 'you are not. Don't you realise you're in the presence of the renowned Deborah Slur?'

Looking at Desadia I say, 'I'm off to the bathroom...'

'I'm coming with you,' she says gripping my hand.

'Hi!' Says Man, I'm here to escort you to the executive bathroom.'

'Where did you...oh! Never mind take them with you, just hurry up about it,' Deborah snarls at Man.

Man smiles at Deborah and says, 'Again I say Hi! And yes we will repair to the bathroom toot suite. I leave you in the hands of Mr Cypher.' Man beckons us to follow him. Which. In fact. We do.

'Deborah,' whispers Louie, 'you have a choice this evening. You may enter one of the four doors of experience situated in each corner of the room. Remember you enter of your own free will. The consequences of this decision are yours and yours alone. Remember also, there is no exit until the door opens to release you.

Your choices are:

Door 1: Pyromania with Nero.

Door 2: Q+A with the Witch-finder General.

Door 3: A guided tour by Tony Blair of his extensive property portfolio.

And finally, no one expects this when they enter

Door 4: Torquemada: the Interview.

I will allow you some time to reach your decision.

Okay, your time is up! CHOOSE!'
Thunderous noise erupts and a bolt of
lightning strikes the stage, Louie appears to
stamp his foot up and down repeatedly.
A waitress clearing tables reported on her FB
page, 'You wouldn't believe it, his feet looked
like hooves.' Her status was updated not long
after this post, which read, 'Gone to
somewhere warmer. But no FB. Lol.'
Louie points to Deborah and says, 'CHOOSE!'
'Well since you insist. Firstly do I want to
sample some coffee in Caffé Nero. Well do I? A
woman of my experience, I think not! And
why oh why a Q+A with a so-called Witch-
finder General. Let's leave this New Age,
getting in touch with your inner woman and
explore Wicca nonsense, to third rate
journalists like Rufus Rabid. Need I go on? I
will anyway, if you had researched me with
any semblance of diligence you would have
realised I am Tony Blair's Guided Tour. Been
there done that Cherié and I, for I am Deborah
Slur, have been friends since I introduced the
Spice Girls to Tony in the 80s. This
introduction paved the way for Tony's
successive election wins and his elevation to
Sainthood.'
'Sainthood!' Queries Louie.
'I mean UN Ambassador for Peace,' says
Deborah executing a polished retraction. ' I
was a frequent house guest of theirs, offering
advice and council on World Affairs. So I don't
think I'll retread old ground. But, Door four,
Torquemada can learn so much from me...'

'SOLD! Says Louie, opening the door, 'after you...'

'Are you not coming?' Deborah asks, feeling a hand on her back which gives her a little shove. As the door closes behind her, she thinks she hears, 'Oh, I'll be there, I'll be th...............!'

'Well!' I say.

'Well, well,! Says Desadia.

'Well!' Smiles Man, 'you could come back in two weeks and collect her. However, that may be a waste of your time as I believe she may be staying longer. And, before you forget, allow me to introduce myself, Hi, I'm Man.'

You are indeed, ' I say, 'do you want to join us for a drink.

'Love to. But I think I may drive the taxi that Vincenzo is currently flagging down to take him home.'

'Man,' says Desadia, you're incorrigible.'

'See you at wedding,' says Louie.

'I'll show you to your carriage,' says Man, 'follow me...'

...finding ourselves at what appears to be a tradesman's entrance to the club, Man gestures into darkness. There is a furious, thunderous galloping and a jet black cab, with red livery identifying it as 'FourHorsemenCabs,' pulls over to us. The cabbie leaning out of his window asks, 'Dave?'

'Yep!'

'Where to?'

'The Rake, Borough Market.'

'Indeed,' says the cabbie opening the door, ' step-inside and before you know it..."

'...we're here, join me for a drink I say, 'before you flight to Berlin.'
'Desadia grins, 'You've read my mind...'

Excerpts from an Artist's (so-called) Life

'...he read my mind,' says Vincenzo shivering.
'Who did,' queries Wanksta©.
'Man did.'
'Let it go,' says Alan, 'we're here to discuss wedding plans. Ms Metro the floor is yours, take it away.'
'Before I do Alan, let's talk about this article from last week's *Guardian*.'
'Er..!' Says Alan
'Er! Indeed,' says Ms Metro opening the paper, and I quote,
'Organised criminals steal the carpet from the floor of the Curzon Cinema in Mayfair. It appears that the gang knew what they were after, as the floor itself was also dug up and removed.
A Spokesman for the Metropolitan Police, James Shirt said, 'It is apparent that the culprits were acting on the instructions of a Mr Big, a Crime Lord, so to speak, and stealing to order.
The Guardian can report that there is a pattern of crime(s) emerging that point to organised and systematic removal of miscellaneous objects from architectural infrastructure to the opportunistic removal of abandoned items.
'There is no no rhyme or reason to these thefts,' Commander Shirt said, adding, 'if I may wax lyrical, it appears as if they've been magicked away. As if,' He continued, 'there was mischief afoot.'

Commander Shirt is currently appearing in the Barking and Dagenham Amateur Dramatic Society's production of 'A Midsummer Nights Dream.

Ms Metro folding the paper closed, stares at Alan and asks, 'Was it you?'

'Er...'

'Er...what?' Says Ms Metro

'Er...'

'Well. Was it?'

'I was told the floor was mine.'

'That was to allow you to have your say, not an invitation to appropriate the floor for a found sculpture installation.

'We've got a wedding coming up and a baby on its way and perhaps, it's time to operate under the radar of law enforcement.'

'Why?' Asks Alan.

'Why what?' Queries Ms Metro.

'Why do I have this theme from Mission Impossible running through my head.'

'Because Alan,' I say, 'you're exhibiting the classic *'Fight or Flight'* response. You're big day is coming up and you are scared...'

'I am Dave.'

Yes you are Alan?'

'That I am Dave.'

'Too true Alan.'

'True indeed Dave.'

'Verily Alan.'

'You are not incorrect Dave.'

'I am not Alan.'

'Respect Dave.'

'Thank you Alan.'

'No, thank you Dave.'

'No, I thank you Alan.'
'No really, thank you Dave.'
'No. Thank you Alan.'
'No. No. I thank you Dave.'
'No. I thank you Alan.'
'And I,' interrupts Ms Metro, 'suggest the pair of you shut the fuck up!'
'Will do,' says Alan.
'I will indeed,' I say.
'We will both shut up, 'says Alan.
'I second that response from Alan,' I say.
'And I, says Alan, 'respect your response.'
'My pleasure,' I say.
'No. It was my pleasure,' says Alan.
'Too kind,' I say.
'So kind of you, Dave, to say so. Thank you.'
'No Alan, it is you who should be thanked.'
'I appreciate your kind words and thank you again.'
'No Alan, I thank you.'
'And I, Dave, thank you.'
'Will the pair of you shut it!
'That was a command, I require no response,' says Ms Metro leaning towards a waiter.
'Yes Miss, are you ready to order?'
'I was born ready!'
'It's true.' Says Alan.
'So very, very true,' I concur.
'Thank you Dave.'
'No, thank you Alan.'
'Don't push me!' Ms Metro says banging the table with a tray of condiments.
'*Rambo?*' queries Alan.

'*First Blood*' although that's tomato ketchup spillage from Ms Metro's tantrum,' I say, passing napkins around to wipe the table.
'Perhaps Dave, it's better described as a hissy fit.'
'It's probably hormonal,' I suggest.
'More probably hysterical Dave.'
'Her emotions are running out of control what with the wedding coming up and planning for the baby.'
'What wedding Dave?'
'Your wedding Alan.'
'Just checking. Thanx. Er..?!?'
'What Alan?'
'Baby?
'You and Ms Metro are having a baby.'
'I knew that.'
'I know you knew that.'
'But thanx for reminding me Dave.'
'My pleasure Alan.'
'The pleasures all mine Dave.'
'Thank you Alan.'
'No thank you Dave.'
'No really thank you.'
'I appreciate your sincerity.'
'No thank you Dave.'
'No Alan, I thank you...'
There is a crash as Ms Metro overturns her table, throws, and fortunately misses Alan with her chair and storms out slamming the doors in her wake.
'One! I say. Well played boys,' comments Clive.
'Superb timing,' says Wanksta©.

'If I may say so, a master-class in timing and repartee,' smiles Nine Mil Phil©, applauding.

'How you say,' says Vincenzo, 'quite the double act.'

'Have I been bad?' Queries Ivanka.

'No,' I say.

'Are you sure Comrade Dave?'

'Yes. Now you and Suzi Uzi© catch up with Ms Metro and take her with you to the Sanctuary in Floral Street. Meet back here at 4pm when we'll unveil the wedding plans and agenda.'

'Da Dave, we go now. And remember Comrade, your mum's a piece of work.'

'The expression Ivanka is *'Mum's the word.'*

'What's the word?' Asks Alan.

'The word on the street is we're not going to continue this duologue, we have wedding surprises to orchestrate. And so little time to complete them. So little time,' I reiterate.

'As usual you surprise me, Dave, with understanding. I thank you.'

'...'

'Dave?'

'...'

'Dave?'

'...'

'Oh I never...what a display of control,' comments Clive.

'Masterful,' confirms Wanksta©, 'Dave played to the net, allowing nothing to get passed him.'

'The Centre Court was witness to a veritable master-class in control,' says AK SE1©.

'What do you say Dave?' Asks Rufus.

'He go to bathroom,' says Vincenzo, 'he say, he was, 'So bored. So terribly, terribly bored.''

Excerpts from an Artist's (so-called) Life

Forty five minutes later, having eaten three cooked breakfasts, a plate of pastries and slurped seven espresso doppios, I exit the dinning room of the Charlotte Street Hotel and...

'Dave.'

'Clive.'

'Don't tell me,' he says, noticing traces of macaron on my chin.

'I'm not going to,' I confirm.

'We can't finalise the plans without you.'

'Let us away then,' I say, 'lead on.'

'Okay,' I say, 'have all public highways, gardens, and other closures been approved by Boris?'

'Check.' Confirms Wanksta©.

'London Borough of Westminster on board?'

'Check.' Confirms AK SE1©.

'Registrar booked?'

'Check.' Confirms Nine Mil Phil©.

'Over to you Alan.'

'Check. You have the ring?'

'Check.'

'Speech prepared.'

'Check.'

'Secret honeymoon destination organised..?'

'Check.'

'...booked, paid for, and transport arranged?'

'Check.'

'Wedding presents of art to be delivered to and/or collected on the day by a team of curators and taken to Clive's gallery?'

'Check.'

'Thanx Dave, is there anything we've not considered?'

'Yes there is. Indeed there is. The possibility of Jake and Dinos bringing flame throwers to the reception, or even the distinct possibility of Dinos haloing into Soho Square with napalm in one hand and a Kalashnikov in the other, lighting himself up and calling in an air-strike on his position.'

'All in the name of art,' says Alan.

'Yes,' I say, 'however who' left to tidy up after him?'

'Point well made Dave. I think we should consider anti-aircraft weapons and a flotilla of Old Bill patrolling the Thames, in boats with Exocet capability.'

'Just to be on the safe side,' I say, 'just to be on the safe side.'

'Secret meeting over? ' asks Alan

'Yes, time for a drink before Ms Metro returns to join us for a drink,' I say.

'Incidentally Dave, where is our honeymoon Destination?'

'Well since you ask, you and Ms Metro will be following in the footsteps of 'Withnail...'

'...and I,' says Ms Metro will be there.'

'And I,' says Ivanka, 'will provide the embrocation.'

'Not a clue,' I say.

'Completely over her head,' confirms Wanksta©.

'Lighter fuel?' Queries Ivanka.

'Let it go,' I say.

'Fork it!'

'No.'

Don't threaten me with a dead fish Comrade.
'No'
'Am I being bad, Comrade Dave.'
'Should we go to your studio, where I will lie over sofa naked, except for my tight black panties, which you will remove by spanking them off, before you administer a strict caning.'
'Ciao,' I say, 'Ivanka and me are leaving, we may be sometime.'
'Groucho later? Asks Alan.
'Yep,' I say, 'Jamie's meeting us there to agree the menu.'
As we leave I hear Clive ask, 'Did you overhear everything Ms Metro?'
'Yes, I thought I'd play along. You don't think I'd really throw a chair at Alan?'
'Ummmmm!' I think.

Excerpts from an Artist's (so-called) Life

As we enter the Groucho, three hours later, Ivanka says loudly, 'I'm still feeling bad, Comrade Dave.'
'Rein it in Ivanka,' I say.
'Put the reins on me and make me!'
'Don't tempt me.'
'Man-up Comrade.'
'Ivanka!'
'Yes Dave.'
'This is not about you.'
'Am I being to bad for you?'
'No.'
'Am I too provocative?'
'No.'
'Will I pay for this later?'
'Yes!'
'That Comrade is music to my ears. The sound of the swish and thwack as the cane sails through the air and lands with a bite on my bottom. My bottom that has been begging for it.'
'Ivanka?'
'Yes Dave.'
'We will continue this later.'
'By Lenin's Ghost we will Comrade.'
'Dave.'
'Alan.'
'Jamie's here, come and join us.'
'Dave?'
'Jamie.'
'Cheap as chips, Dave, cheap as chips!'
'What are..?'
'Chips Dave. Chips.'

'Sorry Jamie,' I say, 'what are you talking about?'

'Chips Dave.'

'Because?'

'Bite size chips Dave, and bite size fish!'

'Er..!'

'Bite size sausage rolls, and bite size burgers!'

'..?'

'Bite size Toad-in-the-Hole...all served on miniature plates, no knives or forks. We're talking *'finger-food'* Dave.'

'..?'

'Bite size wedding cake, perfectly made for every guest...'

'I understand,' I say.

'...and full size bottles of London Pride, with an optional straw for the softly spoken.'

'Dave?'

'Yes Ivanka...'

'Uncle Joe would have approved of this, Petit bourgeois, cooks idea.'

'I believe he would. What does Alan and Ms Metro say Jamie?'

'Don't know, they're quaffing the samples.'

'Where?'

'Up the apples and pears.'

'Let us pay them a visit,' I say, 'my taste buds have been ticked.'

'Oo Er missus,' exclaims Jamie.

'This is the wedding buffet,' says Alan through a mouthful of, at least, eight bite size Toad-in-the-Holes.

'We approve Jamie,' says Ms Metro, spraying us with crumbs from a similar amount of bite sized burgers.

Eschewing the straw(s) I sample fourteen bottles of London Pride. Waking up on the pool table an hour later, I think, 'I need a drink,' and climbing on the back of a passing Vincenzo, I *'Giddy-up,'* him to the bar. Ordering ten bottles of London Pride, I say, ' and no straws.'

'Can't do Dave.'

'Why not Clare.'

'Alan and Ms Metro have told me, in no uncertain terms that until your best-man speech is completed at the wedding you're on a ten drink limit, and you've already passed that.'

'How terribly beastly, I feel quite faint!'

'It won't work, Dave.'

'Clare...'

'Dave.'

'...stop me from falling...'

'I am here Comrade. Come Clare let us carry him to his studio and you can witness an episode of *'Dave and his Bad Girlfriend,'* and if you're bad, I will encourage Dave to introduce you to his sofa.'

'Ivanka!'

'Da Clare.'

'What are we standing around for, let's go.'

'My thoughts exactly,' I say, 'my thoughts exactly.'

'Do what? Do what? My old son, you can't naff off without sampling the wedding day buffet. Which I'm calling *'Jamie's Small is Scrumptious Collection.'* Party food for all occasions, coming soon to an aisle in your local Sainburys. It's what I call, 'cheap as...'

'Jamie?'

'Good old British Nosh.'

'Jamie?'

'To be followed by Italian, French, German, Tex-Mex and a Fusion range of World Foods in miniature. *Jamie's Mini-Me Collection,*' this will sit alongside my new range of conserves *Jamie's Jams.*'

'Jamie,' I say, 'are you using Alan's wedding to Ms Metro as a blatant marketing opportunity?'

'Do me a favour Dave, of course I am.'

'Shall we partake of some Lilliputian morsels?' I query.

'I will give us strength Comrade for a night in your studio.'

Excerpts from an Artist's (so-called) Life

My phone vibrates and starts to play Bonzo Dogs,' *'I'm the Urban Spaceman...'* I open the flip...'Baby, I've got speed,' I say.

'Dave?'

'Clive.'

'Have you heard?'

'Heard what Clive?'

'LBC are reporting that DF, Tim Gauguin, Max Hammer and a number of others have absconded from the Richard Dadd Memorial Hospital for Tired and Emotional Artists.'

'Absconded?'

'Escaped Dave.'

'And this, you believe, interests me because?'

'Of what they wrote on the walls before they escaped.'

'Okay Clive. What did they write on the walls?'

'They scrawled, in what was at first thought to be blood, but subsequently identified by the Police Forensic Unit, as acrylic paint, the words, *'We have a wedding to attend.'*

'Clive, I could be crocheting a spider plant pot holder rather than listen to this pedestrian nonsense.'

'There's more Dave.'

'Clive could you, perchance, get to whatever the point is?'

'Some of the words were crossed out and replaced!'

'With what Clive? Sketches of straight jackets, faux Banksy daubs?'

'No Dave?'
'What does it say?'
'We have a wedding to destroy! Our Manifesto as The Neo-Situationalist Collective is 'Out of Destruction comes Creation.''
'Bored Clive, so terribly, terribly bored.'
'There's more Dave.'
'There always is Clive. Always so much more...'
'They've named a date for their first action piece, the date coincides with Alan and Ms Metro's wedding. Trust me Dave, this is what they'll destroy to announce themselves.'
'What are the Old Bill doing about it?'
'There's nothing they can do.'
'Why not Clive?'
'Other than minor property damage, the Police have limited powers to intervene.'
'Again Clive, why not?'
'Because the absconders were in the psychiatric wing voluntarily, enabling them to leave whenever they wanted. None of the absconders were Sectioned.'
'Clive, it's not unreasonable to describe DF and Max Hammer as sociopaths with delusions of grandeur. What one could reasonably call *'nutters.'*
'Dave, the Metropolitan Police spokesperson, Chief Inspector Shirt said, 'There was no cause for concern to the public, we consider this little more than an *'Art prank.''*
'Did he say anything else Clive?'
'He said that there were a large number of tickets available for the Barking and

Dagenham Amateur Dramatics Society's production of *'On the Waterfront.'*

'Anything relevant, Clive?'

'Apparently the Chief Inspector is having to step in and play the Blanche Dubois part, as the actor(ress) playing Blanche has decided not to tread the boards on this particular production.'

'Chief Inspector Shirt explained that she said, 'She'd sooner be locked in an airless room, in a damp castle on a remote Scottish island, contemplating the inevitability of death rather than share the stage with a troupe that couldn't act their way out of a wet paper bag in a rainstorm.' She continued, 'Furthermore the so-called director, who is also playing the part of Stanley Kowalski, Nigel, knows absolutely nothing about acting or directing, or the theatre for that matter. And his incessant quoting of his alleged intimate conversations with his protégé, Kenneth Brannagh was reason enough to give up not only this production but theatre altogether, her parting words to him were, 'Break a leg or better still your god-damn neck, I'm off to HBO.' She then exited stage right and keep on walking.'

'Clive.'

'Dave?'

'Clive, I understand what she means, let me ask again, did the Chief Inspector say anything relevant to the wedding?'

'Er...'

'Clive,' I say and close the flip. I text Alan and Ms Metro and arrange to rendezvous with the Usual Suspects.

Excerpts from an Artist's (so-called) Life

Patisserie Valerie. 1ˢᵗ floor window tables. 9am.
Roll call: Alan, Ms Metro, Clive, Wanksta©, Vincenzo, Nine Mil Phil©, AK SE1©, Suzi Uzi©, Colin 45©, Ivanka, Rufus Rabid...

'The agenda,' I say, 'is our response to a possible incursion by third rate artists and wannabe Stan Lee's, instigated by DF, and his usual entourage of retainers, distainers and no- brainers, should they try to use the wedding as an opportunity to promote their Situationalist Collective. I'm open to suggestions on how we avoid DF using the wedding as a publicity stunt.'
'Terminate them with maximum fire-power and extreme prejudice,' suggests Nine Mil Phil© channelling Donald Trump.
'More realistically we could employ a face-management team to work security, like we do at the Gallery,' says Clive.
'Whata you say?' Queries Vincenzo.'
'Bouncers,' says Clive.
'Bouncers! Whata you say?'
'Putting it simply Vincenzo, a group of shaven-headed muscle-men in suits three sizes too small, whose sole purpose is to intimidate everyone.'
'How you say,' says Vincenzo, Neanderthal thugs.'
'You've hit the nail on the head,' says Clive.
'It's got my vote,' says Suzi Uzi©.
'And mine,' confirms AK SE1©.

'But,' I say, 'is this the way we want to present, what has been described as the biggest event on the Art Calendar this year, as our attempt to satirise a Northern nightclub on a Saturday evening?'
'Did you spill my pint?' Says a red faced Wanksta©.
'Tosser!' Shouts Nine Mil Phil©.
'You lookin' at my at my bird?' Asks Alan.
'You want some?' Inquires Clive poking Rufus in the chest.
'Wanker,' Shouts AK SE1©.'
'Come on you cant,' spits Suzi Uzi©.
'Fuck you, you cant,' growls Wanksta©.
'You calling me a cant, you fucking cant,' I shout (I just couldn't resist).
'Not the face, not the face!' Cries out Vincenzo.
'You want some, you want a piece of me,' shouts out Rufus kicking over a chair.
'Dave,' says Carol our waitress of the hour.'
'Carol, yes you can pose for me, remember to wear your tightest underwear, you know I do like a challenge...'
'That's not what I want to talk to you about.'
'How terribly beastly...'
'Dave, listen,
'Why? I'm feeling a little petulant...'
'Because you were overheard by a couple of tourists, who happened to be sitting downstairs, not realising this isn't a branch of Starbucks, and thinking you guys were being serious belled the Old Bill...'
'Anna, let me guess this is not about you modelling for me?'

'No, but since you mention it, Carol and me were thinking we could both model for your new *'Tails of a Contemporary Marquis'* series of paintings.'

'Have you been bad,' I ask.

'Very,' says Anna, 'I've forgotten to tell you there are seven Old Bill vehicles outside the Café blocking off Old Compton Street...'

'Dave!'

'Isabel?'

'Dave. Firstly, if you'll allow me to answer the question at the forefront of your mind, they're so tight they look like they've been sprayed on. And secondly,' she says, catching her breath, 'There are 20+ Old Bill outside, tooled up for a barney, ready to subdue everyone in this room.'

'How do you know this? Actually, let me rephrase the question. How the fuck did you come by this information?'

'Anne and Stan, who are on a day trip from Sevenoaks asked me to take their photograph with them poised with forks over one of our pastries, ready to tuck in. While I was setting this up, they overheard...'

'Isabel.'

'Dave?'

'I cannot believe I asked the question...!'

'Anyway Dave, they...'

Any further dialogue is cut short as four Old Bill rushing upstairs trip on the top step and land in a heap. A further nine Old Bill, carrying shields, are unable to stop their momentum, add to the pile. Thirty seven of their colleagues trapped on the stairs, are radioing in, *'Officer Down! Officer Down!'*

There is a muffled, *'Fucking Northern monkey's,'* and, *'Get this fat fuck off me,'* coming from the pile of bodies.

A senior officer in an attempt to regain control and gather a situation report for the Control Unit parked in Dean Street, walks calmly between the mass of officers pepper spraying everyone to the left and right of him as he cuts a swathe up the stairs. Reaching the top, he surveys the devastation, screams into his Motorola, *'Officer Down! Back up required!'* And pepper spraying himself in the face, he jumps and lands on top of the writhing heap of Old Bill.

'Fuck-a-me!' Exclaims Vincenzo.

'Come with us,' whispers Carol. 'We're leaving via the rear exit, Anna will lead.'

'Lead on,' I say, 'let's continue our breakfast/brunch, wedding strategy meeting at Orrery, where we can plan our lunch strategy over the lunch menu. We have had our *amuse bouche* in Patisserie Valerie. It's now time to get serious!'

'What-Is-He-A-Saying?' Asks Vincenzo.

'That we are going to continue our planning in a more conducive milieu,' explains Alan.

'I, er...'

'Go with the flow,' suggests Nine Mil Phil©.

'Who's Flo, she wanna your models?' Vincenzo asks looking decidedly perplexed.

'Anyway moving on,' says Alan, 'I second Dave's plan. Let us pour ourselves into a black-cab and make haste.'

'And you Carol and Anna will be our guests,' I say.
'What about Flo?' Asks Vincenzo.
'Mamma Mia,' exclaims Alan
As we exit Old Compton Street the cabbie asks, 'What's with all the Old Bill?'
'It all revolves around the North/South divide,' I say. 'Northern Monkey's versus Southern Softies, the battle lines have been drawn, it's Oasis v Blur all over again!'
'Do me a favour,' says the cabbie, finally noticing that there's about ten people too in the cab,' I'm not...'
'Say no more,' I say, 'see this as a nice little earner.'
'But there are two..?'
'...Waiter person's in...Says Anna.
'...in the front with me. It's not allowed.
'Then we suggest you continue driving before you get pulled over,' says Carol.

Excerpts from an Artist's (so-called) Life

Slipping the cabbie two perfectly folded £50 notes, we enter Orrery and liberate enough tables to accommodate us.

'We'll start,' I say to the maître d', 'with everything off the lunch menu.'

'You cannot be serious,' he says, looking at me with maître d' disdain.

'He is serious, Comrade, as a nine-tailed cat.' Ivanka says. 'Did you attend the Uncle Joe Academy of Customer Service? Did you hone your, so-called, customer facing skills as a guard in the Gulag system?

Flicking a piece of lint off his cuff he turns and walks away.

'The Comrade waiter is ignoring me, Comrade Dave.'

'He doesn't know what he's missing,' I say as a waiter approaches our table.'

'Bon jour. I have been told by the maître d' to inform you that you and your party are not welcome here and request that you leave the restaurant immediately. Sorry.'

'It's okay,' I say, you're just the messenger. Would you be so good as to ask him to return to our table and explain his unilateral decision.'

'My pleasure,' turning he suddenly stops and looking back says, 'I know!'

'You know what Comrade?' Ivanka queries.

'You're Dave,' he says looking at me. And you must be Ivanka.'

'You are correct Comrade. But who are you?'

'I am Pierre.'

'Your English is perfect,' I say.
'Born in Balham.'
'That, no doubt, accounts for it,' says Alan.
We watch as the maître d' tells Pierre to *'naff off'* and do his job, while he still has one.
Walking into the kitchen Pierre returns with two more waiters carrying six bottles of Prosecco. 'A drink while we wait?' He says orchestrating the filling of glasses.
The maître d' storms over demanding to know, 'Just what do you think you're doing? I told you to throw this lot out!'
Feeling a tap on his shoulder, the maître d' turns around, nods and turning back to us says, 'This is where you get yours. This is the restaurant manager.'
'Hello Nathan,' I say.
'Hi Dave, loved your new exhibition, the girlfriend says when can she...'
'Any time she wants Nathan.'
'What can I do for you?'
'Well...' I start to say...'
'You can throw them out,' interrupts the maître d'.
'Why would I want to do that?' Asks Nathan.
'Because they want to order everything on the lunch menu!'
'And?'
'Because they want to order everything on the lunch menu for lunch.'
'No. Still don't get it.'
'They're taking the piss, what do they think this is?'
'It's a restaurant.'

'Nobody orders the entire menu! They're having a laugh.'

'Do you know who these people are?' Queries Nathan.

'Wankers. That's who they are.' Turning to Pierre and poking him in the chest, he says, 'You. Go to the kitchen and tell the staff the maître d' orders them to come and remove an unwanted presence from the restaurant.'

Pierre looks to Nathan for a cue.

Nathan nods saying, 'Do as the maître d' requests and assemble the staff here, please Pierre.'

Pierre, looking a little crestfallen, walks to the kitchen. Returning two minutes later with the chef, pastry chef, sous chef and three waiters. Nathan, looking at the assembled staff says, 'I have an announcement, with immediate effect Pierre is the new maître d', and your first task is to remove this...

'Fascistic front of house tosser,' suggests Rufus.

'Quite,' nods Nathan.

'Goose-stepping car park attendant,' contributes Suzi Uzi©.

'Failed traffic warden,' I suggest.

'By Putin's sputum,' declares Ivanka, 'you are right! Let them expel him. We must redact his existence!'

'What the fuck do you think you're doing,' the maître d' says as he's surrounded by the staff.

'Showing you the door,' says Pierre.

'You won't get away with this,' he shouts as he's bundled through the restaurant and out the door.

'Bite me!' The sous chef calls after him.

'Eat me!' Shouts the pastry chef, realising too late what he'd said, 'I mean bite me...suck my neck you, you bloodsucker...'

'Give up now,' says Pierre, 'delicate Italian pastries are your forte, leave the rapid fire witticisms to...'

'...Alan,' I say.

'...Dave,' says Alan.

'Enough of this banter,' I say, 'let's order... Pierre we'll have the entire lunch menu, everything off the specials board and twenty five bottles of Prosecco.'

'With pleasure.'

'No Pierre, it is our pleasure to dine in the fine restaurant.'

'The pleasure is enhanced knowing we are cooking for such distinguished bohemians. So I say, on behalf of the staff and myself, thank you!'

'Uh oh!' Says Vincenzo shaking his head.

Nine Mil Phil©, looking to the heavens, says, 'Oh Art! Forgive him, for he knows not what he is getting himself into.'

Wanksta© taking the cork from a bottle of Prosecco, drinks deep and lining up two more bottles in front of him, addresses them, saying, 'Better a bottle in front of me, than a frontal lobotomy.'

Alan crosses his arms, gets himself comfortable and leaning back into his chair says,

'Dave..?'

Taking a breath, ' I say, 'No Pierre. Thank you.'
'No,' says Pierre, 'thank you.'
'No really. Thank you.'
'No thank you.'
'No. I thank you.'
'No really...'

[Editors Note: The next 6.5 pages have been redacted. Refer to the previous chapters or novels in the London Boulevardier series to acquaint yourself with the missing dialogue. You have been warned! 'I thank you for your attention.' 'No really...']

...to be continued in;

**The London Boulevardier
Excerpts from an Artist's
(so-called) Life.
Vol. 5   The Wedding**

www.ingramcontent.com/pod-product-compliance
Lightning Source LLC
Chambersburg PA
CBHW070906180526
45168CB00005B/1945